Bitco..., Ethereum, & Blockchain:

Surprising Insights from 200+ Podcast Interviews of Industry Insiders

by **Richard Jacobs**

Speakeasy Publishing
73-03 Bell Blvd, #10
Oakland Gardens, NY 11364
www.speakeasypublishinginc.com

Ordering Information:

Quantity sales. Special discounts are available on quantity purchases by corporations, associations, and others. For details, contact the publisher at the address above.

Orders by U.S. trade bookstores and wholesalers.

Please contact Speakeasy Publishing:

(888) 991-2766 or visit www.speakeasypublishinginc.com.

Printed in the United States of America.

Published in 2017.

ISBN: 978-1-946481-35-1

FOREWORD

I'm not a developer, nor an industry insider in the Bitcoin & Blockchain ecosystem, BUT... after doing podcast interviews with over 200 companies, consultants, venture capitalists, crypto-journalists, local bitcoin traders, and others in the space, I've learned a thing or two about this fascinating, fast-expanding world.

...and I wanted to share what I've discovered from these interviews, from attending a local, weekly, crypto meetup in Austin, Texas (sponsored by Factom – thank you) for the past year, from attending the BTC Miami and Consensys conferences, and from daily reading of articles published by Coin Telegraph, Coindesk, Bitcoin.com; from YouTube videos by Andreas Antonopoulous, The World Crypto Network, The Crypto Show, The Bitcoin Podcast, and more.

Discovering Bitcoin has led me to question to the nature of money, of governance, of finance, and has opened my eyes to the plight of the world's billions of 'unbanked', to the many uses blockchains are going to play in the future, and to an entire world – a subculture – that is small, but growing fast, and poised to change the world.

Congratulations for being interested enough in "crypto" to forget the mainstream warnings that bitcoin is only used by terrorists and criminals – it's here to stay.

DEDICATION

To Brian Deery, Paul Snow, and David Johnston of Factom – thank you for your patience with me the past year. I must've asked you 10,000 questions, and you answered them all without complaint! Thank you as well for the weekly bitcoin meetup – I've made tons of connections because of it.

To Mate Tokay of Bitcoin.com – thank you for being my very first podcast interviewee and for your continued support during my bitcoin and blockchain journey.

ABOUT THE AUTHOR

Richard Jacobs discovered Bitcoin in 2013, by reading an article in the New York Times, but dismissed the idea as a curiosity (like many).

Fast forward to October 2016, when he started a podcast called "Future Tech Podcast" – the goal was and is to learn about 'round-the-corner' new technologies, such as Artificial Intelligence, 3D printing, stem cells, regenerative medicine, Bitcoin and blockchain (of course), and more.

Since October 2016, Richard has interviewed 400+ different companies and consultants, 200 of which are in the Bitcoin / Ethereum / blockchain space. Richard also attends a weekly local Austin, Texas Bitcoin meetup, sponsored by Factom. He is now a crypto-enthusiast, and small-time hodler.

In February of 2017, Richard joined Bitcoin.com to help run their podcast: Bitcoin – the internet of money.

After interviewing 200 bitcoin / blockchain companies (and counting), Richard's fascination with the industry had grown to a point where he had to "get the information out of his head" and into the hands of other crypto enthusiasts (like you, the reader).

Richard is currently planning and hosting **The Bitcoin, Ethereum & Blockchain Superconference**, to be held in Dallas, Texas, February 16, 17 & 18, 2018. For more info, visit www.BitcoinSuperConference.com or email organizer@bitcoinsuperconference.com

Richard has also partnered with several marketing veterans, and successful startup founders to build a team of 48 people behind his blockchain-focused business development consultancy firm, **Blockchain Edge**. Visit www.BlockchainEdge.net if you are a founder, employee, or member of a blockchain company for business development advice and consulting.

WARNING & DISCLAIMER

The content of this book is purely informational in nature.

Please do not rely upon any of it for investment, tax, or any other type of advice. I am not an accountant, doctor, lawyer, or financial advisor – simply a writer.

All the content herein is based on my experience and non-expert opinion. Am I right? Am I wrong? Only time and circumstance will tell. My views are solely mine and NOT necessarily those of the companies or individuals named herein. Please do not assume nor imply otherwise.

Cryptocurrencies and Blockchain-based Tokens are extremely volatile, they are new, largely unknown, and you should exercise extreme caution when contemplating speculating.

Do your own due diligence, always, and seek the proper professional advice.

Table of Contents

9

13

CHAPTER 1:
WHY DID I WRITE THIS BOOK?

You can decide to have a positive or negative outlook, and to fill your days and thoughts with good thoughts or bad thoughts – to dwell on imminent disasters (most of which never happen) or to get excited about the future.

In May, 2016, I decided to focus more on the positive by subscribing to a weekly email newsletter from Peter Diamandis, founder of the X-Prize. I started getting his weekly emails which showcased near-term future tech, such as advances in stem cell research, bitcoin and blockchain, 3D printing, artificial intelligence, brain computer interfaces, virtual reality, and more.

At the same time, the 2016 United States election was happening – Trump vs. Hillary. Every time I thought about the election, I felt stressed, angry and unhappy. Every email I read from Peter Diamandis, I found interesting new developments and felt excited and intrigued instead.

In October 2016, I started hearing about Bitcoin (after putting it aside for 3 years) and decided that the best way to learn more about near-term future technologies was to create a podcast and interview the actual people who were working on these breakthroughs.

I had no idea where the podcast would take me – I financed its creation on my own, and asked a friend of a friend to help me setting up podcast guests, part time.

The first guest that was willing to talk with me (I had a completely unknown and new podcast) was Mate Tokay, COO of Bitcoin.com. Score! I was elated and felt that I hit the jackpot, right out of the gate with my first podcast.

Sitting in my car, using my cell phone and a recording app, Mate and I talked for 45 minutes and I grilled him with dozens of questions about bitcoin.

After the first podcast, I was more excited than ever, and as the Future Tech podcast built momentum, was able to entice more interviewees, who referred yet more industry players.

I started getting dozens, then hundreds, then thousands of listeners and downloads of the podcast and kept it going. Fast forward to August 2017, I had interviewed over 200 companies and individuals in the Bitcoin, Ethereum, altcoin, cryptocurrency, crypto token and blockchain space. (I could also call it the distributed ledger space and many more names, but you get the idea)

As I was building the podcast I found a local Bitcoin meetup here in Austin, Texas where I live (sponsored and held by Factom). I started going weekly and met crypto-enthusiasts, veterans, newbies, investors, hodlers (I'll define 'hodlers' later), miners, and more.

Factom's gracious hosts are Brian Deery, Paul Snow, David Johnston, and on occasion, other Factom personnel. You'd be amazed at how much they know in the crypto space, and the ongoing patience they demonstrate, week after week, fielding my unending questions and the questions of 30 to 60 other attendees (thank you, guys).

I ended up going to The North American Bitcoin Conference (BTC Miami) in January 2017 and learned a ton from the vendors, speakers and attendees there.

At the conference, I meet some of my podcast heroes, like Paul Puey of Airbitz (very nice, super-knowledgeable tech guy), representatives from Dash Coin, Charlie Shrem, Danny from the Crypto Show (local Austin radio show), a Venezuelan miner (never asked his name for obvious reasons), and many other folks in the crypto ecosystem.

I met with Mate Tokay of Bitcoin.com in person, and it just so happens that they were looking for a new podcast host – about a month later, I was now hosting the Bitcoin.com podcast as well as the Future Tech podcast!

Fast forward to August 2017, and interviewing 2f00+ companies and individuals in the crypto space, I believe I have a very unique perspective and a 30,000-foot view of the landscape of the Bitcoin, alt coin, crypto token and blockchain universe.

I've interviewed mining companies, venture capitalists, alt coin creators, crypto consultants, remittance providers, artificial-intelligence-informed algorithmic crypto traders, payment rail providers, banking the unbanked, smart contract developers and various other actors involved in the space - fascinating to say the least.

After six months and 60+ interviews, I started becoming one of the most knowledgeable people attending my weekly Austin Bitcoin meetup, and decided to write this book – to share what I've learned from interviewing 200+ crypto companies.

That's why I wrote this book.
Now why should YOU read it?

Because the crypto ecosystem has expanded so rapidly, because most folks have day jobs and can't spend all day online researching and watching YouTube videos, and because I have spent so much time discussing products, tokens, and use cases with hundreds of companies, you'll find this book extremely useful as a curation of what's "going on" in the crypto space.

Does this book encompass everything that's going on? Not even close. It's impossible to do so – this space moves so fast, is evolving so quickly, and is growing so fast, this is only a fraction of what's out there. ...but a useful fraction, you'll discover!

I've noticed that people who are interested in this world (crypto enthusiasts) tend to focus only on a sliver of it. Some folks love Bitcoin and that's all they think about (they are called Bitcoin maximalists), others love Ethereum, or Monero or ICOs and that's all they focus on. Some want to mine various coins. Others are busy running startups and by necessity, are focused on their part of the industry.

Whether you want to invest in crypto and the companies that are working to bring their particular use case of blockchain tech to market, or you just want to know more about the industry, this book is intended for curious newbies or even experienced enthusiasts.

Each chapter covers various concepts, and a list at the end contains the 200+ companies I've interviewed.

CHAPTER 2:
THE BASICS OF BITCOIN
AND BLOCKCHAIN

Bitcoin is engineered money. Digital money. A store of value. A medium of exchange. A unit of account. Bitcoin and other cryptocurrencies, just like regular, government-backed money ('fiat'), are mostly electronic. Cash, gold and silver are some of the last holdouts of physical money, although even these assets are only partially physical and are becoming digital.

If you think about the money you have in your bank account, the only reason you have it there, is because the bank's database (ledger) says you do.

Money is an idea; a social agreement.

Let's say you "have" $500 in your bank account. If banking system says you do and is willing to allow you to pay other people electronically, or allows you to withdraw pieces of paper that say they are worth $500, then you "have $500".

But what if your bank gets hacked, or if a judge orders that money to be taken from you, or a corrupt bank updates its ledger? Your bank account simply updates its database to show your new balance of $0.

Where did the money "go"? It went nowhere, because it never existed physically in the first place. It was and is, simply an idea – an agreement by people living under a nation state that you have something of value and an electronic ledger (the bank's database) says you do.

Is Bitcoin (and other crypto tokens) new, strange, and untrustworthy? Perhaps no more so than "real money", especially if you live in Greece, Venezuela, Zimbabwe, India, or dozens of countries that have devalued, stolen, extorted, or manipulated the value or use of what you call "money".

Is Bitcoin used by drug dealers, criminals and

terrorists? Yes. So is cash, in every currency in the world. So are credit and debit cards. So is electronic money (the kind you are using right now). No difference.

Is cryptocurrency the same as "regular money"? Yes and no. Let's examine the details of why Bitcoin and other crypto tokens are so fascinating, revolutionary, and game changing.

Public Ledgers

In the United States, fiat currencies use physical cash, checks, wires, ACH withdrawals, account to account transfers, online bill pay, Paypal, Venmo, credit, debits, hand to hand live exchanges of cash, and more to conduct transactions. Some of these methods of money transfer or holdings (ex: cash) can be completely anonymous – they won't be listed on any accounting ledger. Not so with Bitcoin and other blockchain-based crypto token systems.

Bitcoin, for instance, utilizes what is called a distributed ledger to show every single transaction that has ever occurred using Bitcoin. There is no "cash" equivalent of Bitcoin, nor is there physical Bitcoin you can hand to someone.

A ledger is a listing of who has what. For example, let's stay Bitcoin only has ever had 3 transactions this far. The ledger would show the following:

Transaction 1: Satoshi starts the ledger with 100 bitcoins, which are 'held' at an address he owns / controls.

Transaction 2: Satoshi sends 10 bitcoins to Sally – the Bitcoin ledger now shows that Satoshi has 90 BTC and Sally has 10 BTC.

Transaction 3: Sally sends 5 BTC to Joe. Satoshi still has 90 BTC; Sally 5 BTC; Joe 5 BTC.

As of this writing, approximately 200 million transactions have occurred using Bitcoin, and the Bitcoin full ledger lists <u>every single one of them</u>.

Bitcoin appears to be transferrable from person to person (i.e. I send Bitcoin from my address to your bitcoin address), but what is actually happening is this:

When Satoshi transfers 10 BTC to Sally, as in the example above, the Bitcoin ledger updates to show this transaction. Bitcoins are not "moving from place to place". Nothing is moving – the master ledger is simply being updated with new information.

The previous state of the ledger – i.e. when Satoshi had 100 BTC, before he transferred 10 of them to Sally, still exists and is memorialized forever on the ledger. Now the ledger shows Satoshi had 100 BTC, and then shows that Satoshi "sent" 10 BTC to Sally and now "has" 90 BTC.

If you used block explorer software (yes, this really exists) and look at today's full Bitcoin ledger, you would be able to see every transaction that has ever occurred, and calculate / know the previous state(s) of every address.

Distributed Ledgers

The Bitcoin ledger is distributed, (as are other public blockchains). This means that an exact copy of its ledger exists on thousands of different computers all around the world.

Because Bitcoin's software protocol has a mechanism to check if everyone ledger holder (full node) agrees that they have the same ledger with all the same transactions in it, there's no way to "take down the network" by attacking a few computers.

Destroying one or two or 500 computers would not destroy the network or the ledger, because it is distributed and decentralized over thousands of computers worldwide.

This means no government, no nation-state, no single actor has the capacity to take down the Bitcoin network and burn the ledger. The ledger is public, viewable, and distributed world-wide.

Blockchain Ledger Transactions Can't Be Undone, Nor Their History Altered

Transactions are grouped into blocks of data and posted to the Bitcoin ledger every 10 minutes, 24 hours a day, 7 days a week, 365 days a year.

Once a block of data is posted to the ledger, it cannot be altered or removed (actually, it could, but this would take unbelievable amounts of computing power to do so and tons of money and is nearly completely unfeasible).

Miners (we will cover mining later) compete for **the right** to post a given block of transactions to the Bitcoin blockchain, by competing to solve a mathematical puzzle every 10 minutes.

Whichever miner or mining operation solves the math puzzle the fastest, wins the race. The Bitcoin network then confirms that the particular miner's solution is valid, and the miner earns the right to add a block of transactions to the blockchain. The winning miner then earns two kinds of rewards:

1. New Bitcoins are created by the Bitcoin protocol (currently 12.5 BTC created per new block, every 10 minutes) and given to the winning miner, and

2. The transaction fees associated with every transaction in the winning block are also awarded to the winning miner.

Why is this important? Because of the effort put in by competing miners and the mathematical difficulty of solving the puzzle, the electricity expended to run computers to solve the puzzle, the time taken, the computational power needed, AND the cryptography used, it's simply "not worth it" and nearly impossible for someone to try to change the ledger's contents once a block has been mined and added to the ledger.

The miners are being rewarded for their work – called "proof of work".

To make matters better (not worse), each successive block in the blockchain is mathematically linked to the previous blocks. If a bad guy tries to <u>alter one single bit of data</u> of any of the blocks, the entire ledger falls apart.

For example: transaction #25,684 is linked mathematically (cryptographically) to transaction #25,683, to #19,694, to #9,334, to #2, and to every single transaction that came before it.

The nature of this linking, and the math involved, is such that if you tried to change a single bit of just one of the transactions, like a Jenga® tower, the whole blockchain will collapse (or show completely wrong information).

THIS is why the Bitcoin blockchain is considered to be tamper-proof, its history un-alterable (called "immutable"), and because it uses a distributed ledger, the entire world can know and verify that a transaction or series of transactions did, in fact, take place.

Why immutable, tamper-proof, distributed ledgers are so valuable

(1) *You can't double-spend* your Bitcoin. If you have 1 BTC, you can't pay someone that 1 BTC, then turn around and try to pay someone else with that same 1 BTC – once you've spent your Bitcoin, you've spent them.

(2) *The past can't be changed* to steal your Bitcoin. No one can monkey with the Bitcoin ledger and change the money associated with an address you control (unless someone gets their hands on your private key).

Even if a government or nation-state, or judge demanded that you 'hand over' your Bitcoin, without your private key, no one could steal it. No one could say, "listen world, Miss Jane Smith no longer has 10 BTC in her wallet – please change the record".

Yes, a judge or powerful entity COULD put a metaphorical gun to your head (through litigation, court order, threat of imprisonment, or even death) and force you to agree to transfer your Bitcoin to them, or surrender your private keys. However, the moment your Bitcoin is transferred from your wallet, that transaction, in order to be valid, is recorded on the Bitcoin blockchain for all the world to see – the old transaction is there as well when you previously had the money in your wallet.

Note: so far, I've been mentioning Bitcoin only, however these same facts and features are true for many (not all) blockchain-based tokens, not just Bitcoin.

More reasons that immutable, tamper-proof, public, distributed ledgers are going to change the world will be discussed later under "other use cases".

For example: imagine all the real estate for a given nation was recorded on a public blockchain. People could own, control, rent, buy, and sell real property (homes, apartments, land, etc) and be sure that their land or their home could not be stolen from them without the world knowing what had happened. The theft could not be hidden.

(3) *You don't have to trust* the person, company, or entity you are transacting with, yet you can still transact with them (i.e. no refunds, no going back once a transaction is complete).

Let's say you and I agree that I will sell you a bag of pistachios for 0.005 BTC (5 milli-bits). You send 0.005

BTC to my address / wallet from your address, I hand you the pistachios, and you walk out the door.

Two days later, after eating the pistachios, you decide that they tasted like crap and you want your money back. You have no recourse. You can't file a chargeback on your VISA or Mastercard credit card. You can't call up your bank and claim that the pistachios were no good and you want your money back. If this were a fiat currency transaction, all the above could happen.

In Bitcoin, there are no refunds unless the recipient of your BTC agrees to refund it. Is this a good thing or a bad thing? Depends on who you ask and on the situation, but it allows for part of your transaction to be trustless.

Huh? What happens if the person I bought the pistachios from truly did sell me rotten pistachios? The trustless part of the transaction was the money you gave to the merchant for the nuts. The merchant could feel 100% safe that the BTC you sent to them, once received, were real and could not be taken from them.

If you had stayed in the store and eaten a few pistachios, there is nothing disputable about the transaction – it is final and did not require a 3rd party escrow company, merchant account, or arbiter to ensure the parties in the transaction trusted each other.

Wait a minute, you may be thinking – this seems WORSE than our current situation when transacting in fiat. If you exercise even a moderate amount of care when transacting with others, even if they are halfway around the world, having the certainty of an un-alterable, un-rescindable transaction has a lot of benefits.

(4) *Peer to Peer (P2P) Transactions* - I can meet you physically and hand you cash. I can send you cash in the mail (although it's very likely to be stolen). Can I deposit cash into your bank account? In many places, no – I would be considered to be a terrorist or criminal for some reason if I want to do that, even if I want to deposit twenty bucks into your bank account.

Can I accept money from you, or from my friends or family through my bank account? Yes, but it often takes days of time and has to be classified as "bill pay", or in some cases, a gift.

The IRS wants to know when this happens. Fees are often applied. Transfers may be denied. If the person I'm sending money to doesn't have an account, or has an account with a different bank, the whole process may be a nightmare or impossible.

I highly doubt most people, upon reading the above, would consider this to be reasonable. Now imagine a "cashless" society that some politicians and governments are pushing for.

Imagine a 3rd party (government, nation-state, financial institution) getting in the way of every transaction you want to make, extracting fees from every transaction, taxing you, surveilling you, scoring your transaction and your behavior against a 'is this person a terrorist or criminal' scorecard, graciously "allowing you" to transfer money... or not.

In happy contrast, you can send Bitcoin to, and receive bitcoin from, anyone in the world, at any time, for any amount, without having to get the permission of a bank, financial institution, government, or nation-state.

I'm not going to advocate you doing this or not. I'm not going to tell you to report each transaction to your local authority or not. I'm not going to tell you that it's safe to transfer your cryptocurrency, or that you can get it back in case there's a problem.

I'm simply stating the benefits of cryptocurrencies (like Bitcoin) that I see – and cheap, peer-to-peer, extremely fast money transfers are a big benefit.

(5) *Anti-inflationary Currency* – most governments can and do 'print' (or simply issue) additional currency when they wish to pay debts, increase the money supply to stimulate lending, borrowing investing and spending, or manipulate the currency and monetary policies of their nation.

Unfortunately, this causes inflation, which dilutes the spending power of existing currency because more money available means your existing money has less value.

Bitcoin, according to its protocol, will only issue 21 million bitcoins ever. So far, approximately 16 f million bitcoins have been mined, and the mining reward halves every four years. The last amount of Bitcoin that will ever be mined will occur in the year 2130 or thereabouts.

This means Bitcoin has a controlled, low-inflationary issuance. It cannot be wildly printed and inflated by any given government – in fact, because thousands (and this is just a ballpark) of Bitcoins have been lost because of carelessness and other reasons, and as more people own and transact Bitcoin, the currency is deflationary. Bitcoin's value may increase dramatically over time, possibly to many times its value today (no guarantees nor investment advice here, folks).

(6) *Fungibility* – If I have a 100 Euro note in my hand and you have a 100 Euro note, are both notes worth the same amount? Which note is better? Neither – and that is fungibility – each US dollar, each Euro, each note or digital amount of fiat money is the same – it can be spent and swapped with other money. There are no recognized differences amongst units of fiat currency.

Thankfully, Bitcoin is fungible as well. My Bitcoin is just as spendable as your Bitcoin and can buy the same amount of goods or services – Bitcoin is interchangeable, just like fiat.

(7) *Divisability* – Each Bitcoin can be divided into 100 million bits, called Satoshis (i.e. each Bitcoin can be displayed up to eight decimal places. Ex: 0.12345678 BTC) This makes it a lot more divisible than regular money.

For example, in the United States, the penny ($0.01 or 1 cent) is the smallest denomination of money. Even a whole dollar is worth very little, and due to inflation, is worth less and less every year.

However, at the time this book was written, one single Bitcoin was worth approximately $4,200 USD, and if you divided that number by 100,000,000, you would get $0.000042, which is simply considered to be zero in the United States (and most countries).

Let's say I want to buy a Starbucks® Pumpkin Spice Latte; I can pay 1 milli bit for it (0.001 BTC ~ $4.20 USD). This leaves a ton of room for the price of a single Bitcoin to reach $10,000, $100,000, or even one million USD. At $100,000 per Bitcoin, I can simply buy that same cup of coffee for (0.000042 BTC ~ 4.20 USD ~ 4.2 micro bits ~ 4,200 Satoshis).

Thankfully, 'denominations' of Bitcoin have names, but there will likely be a need for more names in the future.

So far, you can express Bitcoin in: Bitcoin, milliBits, microBits, and Satoshis, but just like the US dollar and other fiat currencies, it would be useful to have more names similar to quarters, nickels, dimes, or even pence.

To be perfectly clear, you don't have to buy an entire Bitcoin – you can buy and transact in milliBits, microBits, tenths of a Bitcoin, or even in Satoshis (although transaction fees make moving a few Satoshis not worth it – amounts this small are commonly referred to as "dust" transactions).

The human brain doesn't like to work with fractions or numbers that have more than two decimal places. Imagine going to a store and seeing a bunch of bananas priced at 0.000032 BTC. Would you buy it, or balk and think, "how much is that in my currency?"

The divisibility of Bitcoin to eight decimal places also allows for the possibility of charging tiny amounts of money for certain applications, such as micro payments. I can choose, for instance, to charge viewers of my instructional video on knitting a sweater 1 cent apiece, or I can choose to charge them 1/10th of a cent, or 1/100th of a cent and represent those amounts in BTC (ex: 0.1 cent = 0.0000042 BTC)

These seven items are just <u>some of the elements</u> that make cryptocurrency so attractive, useful, game-changing, and different from traditional money. Bitcoin and other cryptocurrencies are poised to possibly become global, digital currencies.

How Much Does The Average Person Need To Know To Use Bitcoin or Blockchain?

Bitcoin and blockchain technology is an amalgamation of many different technologies, assembled and tweaked by Satoshi Nakamoto, yet originally created by nerds, cypher punks, cryptography enthusiasts, computer scientists and programmers.

It IS a long and difficult process to understand Bitcoin and blockchain. In fact, my estimate is that less than 0.1% of the world's population knows much about it, much less deeply understands it. It took me about 30 interviews of companies in this space, and attending the same number of meetups to get a grasp on many of the concepts.

You may laugh, but out of the 200+ interviews I've done of companies in this space, there's 15-20 of them that, after interviewing them for thirty minutes, I STILL came away from the conversation not understanding what they do.

Many people use buzz words like blockchain, distributed, decentralized, peer to peer, crypto currency, tokens, hard forks, consensus mechanisms, and more – many of these people talk without a clear understanding of what they're actually saying.

I've taken it upon myself to interview the companies detailed in this book, to ask follow-up questions, to drill down and get clear, basic, easy-to-understand explanations of what they do. That's also the goal of this book – to communicate clearly to you, the reader, what I learned from interviewing 200+ companies, and spending hundreds of hours learning this space.

Why Marketing Is Critical In The Blockchain Space?

Because of my eight years of experience in marketing, I think this entire industry desperately needs marketing and communications experts to boil down the technology to a real basic level so even your grandmother can use and understand it. If not, it's going to slow and cripple the adoption of blockchain technology and blockchain assets, which I, and you, the reader, don't want.

You and I likely want blockchain technology to go global and to change the world for the better. However, people must realize that unless this technology is understandable to the common person it's going to be an uphill, multi-decade battle of adoption.

A lot of companies ignore this simple fact, but some do get it like Abra, PayCase and Bitpay. These companies, for example, strive to make it feel like their users are not even using bitcoin or blockchain.

Their assumption, perhaps rightly so, is that people don't care about the underlying technologies. They don't want to know. They shouldn't have to figure out how to manage private keys, to write down their 12 word wallet recovery seed, asymmetric cryptography, immutability, decentralized public ledgers, wallets, fiat gateways, and more.

People should be able to send money to their

grandmother in Thailand, without middlemen extorting exorbitant fees, without having to have a bank account, without taking a bus to the local Western Union or Money Gram store, without having to show their ID and sign an affidavit that they're not a terrorist, or using their money to fund crime, without the recipient fearing being robbed outside the store where they pick up cash.

Is that so much to ask? Companies like Bitpay, who helps merchants accept Bitcoin and settles their merchant accounts in fiat, or in Bitcoin (merchant's choice) are helping to facilitate thousands and eventually millions of stores, to accept Bitcoin.

Abra and Paycase are enabling people to send money to whomever they choose, without all the hindrances I listed in the Thailand grandmother example above. The people sending and receiving don't even know that Bitcoin is being used as a payment rail – all they know is that they can now send and receive money using their smartphone, and the transactions are a pleasure vs. the maze of problems they're currently enduring with current money transfer systems.

How to Learn More: Bitcoin & Blockchain Education Resources

There are many resources available for anyone interested in learning more about bitcoin, blockchain and the underlying technologies in this arena.

<u>Here's a short list of resources:</u>

- Telegram channels

- Slack channels

- Podcasts (such as Future Tech Podcast, The World Crypto Network, The Crypto Show, and more)

- Reddit (watch out for trolls!)

- Bitcoin Talk Forums / other forums

- YouTube Videos

- Developer blogs

- Twitter

- Google alerts

- Crypto media outlets (Coindesk, Coin Telegraph, The Merkle, Bitcoin.com, and more)

- Attending live, local meetups where you can interact

with hodlers (yes, I will define this term soon), investors, developers, and other crypto enthusiasts

In addition to the resources listed above, for college and high school students, there is the Blockchain Education Network (BEN). They aim educate get high school, college and university students who are interested in bitcoin, blockchain technology, software development, and entrepreneurship.

BEN has clubs at various high schools and universities all over the world where students get together and learn about cryptocurrency and blockchain technologies.

BEN sponsors hackathons, where teams or individual programmers get together to come up with a solution or new product that uses blockchain technology.

Winners of these hackathons receive prizes which range from cash bounties (paid in crypto), a signed book, invitations to pitch venture capitalists, and often, funding and mentorship of their products.

Some hackathon contestants become real companies that attract venture capital and other investment, such as Distributed ID.

Because BEN is focused on bringing together and educating today's youth, it provides a great service. The kids, high school and university students are the future of blockchain and of our world – kids must be included and learn about these innovations.

CHAPTER 3:

HOW TO BUY, SELL, SEND, RECEIVE, AND 'HODL' (HOLD) BITCOIN

Where to Buy Bitcoin

So how you get your hands on Bitcoin? Where do you buy Bitcoin, Ethereum or other crypto tokens? Until it becomes more widespread, as of right now, finding Bitcoin is a bit tricky, and there are barriers.

For the most part, you can't walk into your local bank branch and try to buy Bitcoin. You can't get it from most local currency exchanges (I approached several currency exchanges in airports in different countries and asked if they sell Bitcoin – the counterperson each time gave me a smug smile and said, "No.").

One way to get Bitcoin is to work for a company that pays you in Bitcoin or some other cryptocurrency. When I worked for Bitcoin.com, once a month they sent money to my Bitcoin wallet. Let me tell you - getting paid in Bitcoin is a thrill!

Another way to obtain cryptocurrency is to meet up with someone in person and to exchange fiat for Bitcoin.

Buying / Selling Crypto in Person

Let's say I have $500 and I want to buy Bitcoin. I meet up with a seller at the local coffee shop. I give my $500 to the seller, and the seller scans the QR code of my public address or types in my public key into their smartphone wallet application, and transfers the requisite amount of Bitcoin into my wallet on my smartphone. Wait 5-10 minutes for the network to confirm the transaction, and we're done!

The largest website, available in 100+ countries, that brings crypto buyers and sellers together is called **LocalBitcoins.com.**

The number of transactions they handle has been exploding, especially in countries where capital controls and governments have been trying to clamp down on Bitcoin. Places like India, China, Russia, even Venezuela and Argentina have seen their local bitcoin trading volume surge tremendously, especially when regulation or a crackdown comes.

Japan, on the other hand, has been experiencing the same surge, but for different reasons. Japan has decided to regulate Bitcoin and other Blockchain assets in a welcoming, fair and equitable manner.

The Japanese government has been proactive and is actively encouraging the use of cryptocurrency. There, local Bitcoin trading is surging not out of fear, but instead from excitement. Hundreds of thousands of merchants are now adopting Bitcoin in Japan as well.

Bitcoin ATMs

Another avenue in which to obtain bitcoin is through Bitcoin ATMs, which are popping up in various cities around the United States and now in other countries.

To use a Bitcoin ATM, you show your ID to the ATM, put your fiat currency in, and the machine will send bitcoin to the wallet of your choosing. Because Bitcoin ATMs are subject to AML / KYC compliance, more than likely you will have to show identification and verify who you are before you can use a Bitcoin ATM.

We'll cover more ways to obtain and sell crypto tokens shortly. You've heard me mention wallets and private and public keys several times now – before we continue to cover how to buy, sell, hodl (hold), trade, and transact crypto, it's vital to talk about wallets.

Wallets

Similar to a physical wallet, a crypto wallet can be (depending on whether you control your private keys) a secure place used to keep digital currencies and app tokens like Bitcoin, Ethereum, Litecoin, Stratis, Zcash, Augur, Gnosis, Golem and many others.

Some wallets only allow you to store Bitcoin, others serve multiple tokens, like Jaxx will allow you hold multiple coins including Bitcoin, Ethereum, Ethereum Classic, Auger, ZCash, Dash and more.

A wallet is software that lives on your smartphone (iPhone or Android app) or on your laptop. Wallets can also be physical devices, called hard wallets, that look like armored USB sticks. Two examples are Trezor and the Nano-S.

Just like a wallet in your pocket that holds cash and credit cards, crypto wallets are named that way to give you the impression that you are storing and protecting your bitcoin and other blockchain assets in them.

The funny thing is that your wallet doesn't actually **store** anything of value. There's no "money" inside of your wallet.

A better metaphor is a keychain (thank you Andreas Antonopolous) on which you hang your public and private keys to one or more addresses (accounts) that only you have acccss to.

Inside of a software wallet, you'll typically see two sets of features:

- Send / Receive

- Buy / Sell

Send / receive allows you to send Bitcoin to or receive Bitcoin from other peoples' wallets. Don't confuse this with [**buy / sell**], which is available only in certain wallets that act as Fiat Gateways (I'll define this later), such as Airbitz and Coinbase. We'll discuss why Buy / Sell is much less common than send / receive shortly.

Send / Receive vs. Buy / Sell

I need to go into detail about [send / receive] versus [buy / sell] because these two options are completely different and the distinction can be confusing.

Send / Receive

Send / receive allows you to send crypto from your wallet to someone else's wallet, or to ask someone to send you crypto FROM their wallet to yours (receive it).

Send / receive is a <u>wallet to wallet transfer</u> of crypto. It may be obvious, but you can't send fiat currency from your wallet to someone else's wallet – you can only send blockchain tokens like Bitcoin.

You can send or receive Bitcoin, Ethereum, or any other token that your wallet supports. Some wallets only support Bitcoin, other wallets support multiple app tokens such as Jaxx, Exodus, Coinomi, and more. Unfortunately, as of this writing, there are no "universal wallets". I wish there were.

Sending

To send crypto from your wallet, you will need the public key of the person you're sending it to. A person's public key is also called their address.

Once you enter the amount of bitcoin you want to send into your wallet (ex: send 0.35 BTC), you'll also be asked to input the recipient's public key manually, or by scanning a QR code representation of their public key.

Once you enter in the recipient's public key and the amount you want to send, you may be asked to confirm the transaction by touching a button, or entering in 2FA – two-factor authentication. If you have 2FA enabled (HIGHLY recommended), you will then either get a code texted to your Smartphone (or enter in a Google Authenticator or other 2FA service key) to verify it's really you and that you really DO intend to send crypto to another wallet. We'll cover two-factor authentication more later.

Receiving

To receive crypto from someone else, you typically don't have to do anything inside your wallet. In some wallets, you will have to first create a public key, or address, to where people can send you crypto. You then provide the sender with YOUR public key (manually or by QR code), then wait for the incoming funds to appear in your wallet as pending or confirmed.

Depending on the blockchain token you're transacting, the send / receive process can take a few seconds, up to 10 minutes (Bitcoin), or sometimes longer if network congestion is high at the time you're sending.

Buy / Sell

Buy / sell means you are using fiat to buy a crypto token, or selling your tokens in return for fiat currency. A small subset of wallets and exchanges allow users to 'cross the fiat chasm' and move in and out of fiat into crypto. These services are called fiat gateways.

Buying

Starting with fiat currency; Euros, US Dollars, or whatever your currency may be, you will be using it to buy crypto (Bitcoin, etc). A majority of the time, you'll be buying Bitcoin, not other tokens, because most fiat gateways are set up between Bitcoin and various fiat currencies. For example, if you wanted to buy Dash you'd often first have to use your fiat to buy bitcoin, THEN exchange your bitcoin for Dash.

Why? Because Bitcoin is used as the reserve currency for most transactions, then Ethereum, then Litecoin, and more rarely, other tokens like Ripple.

Selling

When selling your crypto back into fiat, since Bitcoin is the most common reserve currency, you may have to first sell your token and buy Bitcoin, then sell your Bitcoin and buy fiat.

Bitcoin not only is the major reserve currency for crypto to fiat transactions, but many services have sprung up to help people return to the fiat world from the crypto world, by offering fiat gateways that include direct deposit into your bank account, ACH, bank wire, and more.

Some examples are Coinbase, Gemini, Kraken, Poloniex, Airbitz wallet (which uses Glidera, owned by Kraken) and other exchanges.

Several companies like Bitpay and Coinbase offer pre-paid debit or credit cards that you can load with Bitcoin. Once you send Bitcoin to your card, it's converted into fiat currency and you can use the card with any merchant that accepts credit or debit transactions.

Why Fiat Gateways Are Rare

Very few wallets and providers have buy and sell capabilities. Most allow only send / receive transactions.

Why? Because crossing in and out of fiat is where you touch the third rail of regulations. Governments in nearly every nation on earth exert control over their government-issued, electronic fiat currency – who can buy, who can sell, how much can be transferred, how often, for what amounts, when paperwork is needed to document 'suspicious' transactions, and more.

When you're crossing the bridge from fiat to crypto or crypto to Fiat, many regulations will apply to the company that's allowing you to do this. This is where you run into AML/KYC (anti-money laundering and know-your-customer) requirements; money transmitter licensing; categorization as a money service business; and more.

Because of regulation, wallet providers or exchanges that offer fiat gateways are required to have you verify yourself with a government-issued ID, provide banking and other information to be able to use their fiat gateway.

Exchanges and wallet providers will provide tiered levels of access based on the credentials and account verification you present. For example, if you want to buy more than $3,000 USD in crypto or withdraw more than $3,000 from an exchange per day, you may be required to provide enhanced verification to upgrade your account.

Sadly, you already know how difficult it can be to pay people with your own currency, move your own money around, or withdraw it from a bank. You can't just pay someone from your bank account to their bank account very easily. There are fees involved and it may take hours or days to do it. You may even be blocked from paying someone for various reasons.

To add insult to injury, banks and other financial institutions have an obligation to report what they consider to be suspicious or large transactions.

The simple act of paying someone: be it your brother, mother, sister, individual or company for a service – is monitored, sometimes censored, a fee is taken, taxes may be assessed, and your activity is documented.

Unfortunately, navigating the crypto world can be very confusing and difficult, especially when you're brought right back into the world of fiat and its delays, costs, compliance, surveillance, and regulation.

These facts are not made clear by any wallet that I know of and that's why it's so vital to understand the difference between buy / sell vs. send / receive.

Backup Up or Recovering a Lost Wallet - Seeds

When you're setting up your wallet for the first time, you may be prompted to write down a twelve word 'seed' and store it for safekeeping. Seeds are lists of 12-24 words that can be used to re-generate your public and private keys in the event your wallet is deleted or lost.

As most wallets will tell you, storing your seed securely is one of the single most important things you can do, if you don't wish to lose hundreds or thousands of dollars of crypto that you may own.

What can go wrong? Computers break. Laptops or smartphones fall into toilets, are left behind on airplanes, are stolen, or simply break.

Let's say your smartphone gets stolen. Hopefully whoever stole it can't gain access to your wallet without a passcode and two-factor authentication. You've remotely locked your phone, and everything appears to be safe. You get a new phone, download the wallet app, and sign in…

…and you're told that because you're using the wallet from a previously unknown device, you must provide your seed to recover it. Good thing you wrote down your seed on a piece of paper and stored it in a safe place (not on the same smartphone that was stolen!). Perhaps you even memorized it.

You then enter the 12-word seed into your wallet, and voila! Your address(es) are restored, and you're back in business. The $10,000 in BTC and $2,000 in ETH you held are back in your control.

Just like there is no crying in baseball (as Tom Hanks said in the movies), there are no refunds nor second chances in crypto if you lose your private keys or forget your wallet recovery seed.

Brain Wallets

Some people believe that by choosing the words that compose their twelve-word seed, they can both remember it more easily and keep their wallets protected. This is called a brain wallet, and is not advisable to do, because people are known to use patterns in the way they create their brain wallet, making it easy to hack. It's far better to have a randomly generated seed.

Two-Factor Authentication (2FA)

A lot of wallets will use a login and a password or pin to access them. This is good, however, having two-factor authentication can make your wallets and crypto holdings a LOT more secure.

In two-factor authentication (2FA), your login and password / pin which is the first factor. The second factor can be:

a. an email sent from your wallet that you have to click on to confirm access, or

b. a text sent to your phone number with a code you enter in, or

c. a code provided by Google Authenticator, Authy, or other 2FA apps.

Both factors in 2FA are required to gain access to your account. That makes it a lot safer versus using just a login and a password, which can easily be hacked.

Taking 2FA further, some wallets also offer encryption of your private keys. That means they don't store naked, unencrypted text-based keys on your wallet which adds yet another layer of security.

Hardware wallets store your private keys physically on an isolated microchip that exists inside of the physical wallet (ex: Trezor and Nano-s).

You can also use a paper wallet. This means you

write down your private key(s) on a piece of paper and store that paper securely somewhere.

The Ideal Way to Manage Private Keys and Keep Your Crypto Safe

Unfortunately, there's no ideal way to secure your wallets and manage your private keys. Recently there have also been social engineering hacks against high-net-worth crypto hodlers.

In one story, a hacker was suspicious that someone had approximately two million USD worth of crypto. The hacker called the person's cell phone company and had their phone number ported (changed) to a phone that the hacker owned.

Even though the victim in this case, had two-factor SMS authentication, it backfired on the victim. Because the phone number has been changed to the hacker's burner phone#, the hacker logged into the victim's wallet, received a SMS text message to confirm, confirmed the access code, and gained access to the wallet. He then sent (stole) all of the victim's Bitcoin from their wallet to addresses the hacker controlled. Terrible, but true.

In another incident, someone posted on Reddit a moral dilemma they faced, when a friend of theirs left a paper out in the open that apparently contained their 12-word wallet recovery seed. This person knew that their friend had approximately $90,000 in crypto holdings, and was debating whether to steal it from them. Worst of all, instead of universally condemning the thought, people on Reddit instead said, "finders keepers, losers weepers".

Public / Private Key Pairs

I won't go into asymmetric cryptography which governs the underlying principles of public / private key pairs, except for a few details. You can either manually create a public / private key pair, or your wallet software can do it for you.

As its name implies, your public key is publicly shared, and can be used by anyone to send crypto tokens to you (your address).

In order to **receive crypto from** someone else to your wallet, your public key will suffice, however to SEND crypto held at a given address to another address – i.e. to 'spend' the Bitcoin (or other token) you control, you must use your private key.

Because of the math involved and the unbelievably tremendous computational power required to try to calculate a corresponding private key from public key (read: nearly impossible) he who has the private key to an address controls the funds associated with that address, and so long as the private key has not been stolen, the funds associated with a given address cannot be moved or taken.

There are some downsides to the extreme security of asymmetric cryptography and private keys, however. There have been many instances where a private key has been lost accidentally, and in most cases, that's the end of the story – the money associated with an address that has no private key is locked, or stuck at that address and is un-spendable forever.

Without your private key, even if you have a million bitcoins in a wallet, you'll have no ability to access it, and there's no one you can appeal to (except the math gods) to restore your private key.

Private Key Management

Since your private key(s) are vital to your control of your tokens, what is the best way to keep them safe from prying eyes, thieves, or loss? Should you keep your private keys on your smart phone? How about writing them down on a piece of paper and storing that paper in a bank vault? What about breaking up your private key into pieces and giving those pieces to multiple friends to hold for you?

As you'd suspect, it's not at all easy to keep your private keys safe, and each method has its positives and negatives. When you consider that many people use multiple addresses to store their cryptocurrency, and have multiple wallets for various crypto tokens, things become even more complicated. Now you have to keep track of multiple private keys!

How about using a seed as a backup to store your private keys? Great idea, but now you must protect that seed just like you would protect your keys.

Instead of using paper or multiple backups of your private keys or seeds on computers, you can also use hardware wallets and place the hardware wallets in multiple safe locations as well.

Encrypting your private keys

An even more sensible and secure way to store your private keys is to encrypt them with a passcode or password. Obviously, your password should be secure, and contain capital and lowercase letters, numbers, symbols, and be at least 10 – 20 characters long, but this creates yet another problem... What if you lose your passcode and can't unlock your private keys?

Multi Signature Wallets (multi-sig)

Some wallets or protocols require 2 out of 3 signatures, or 3 out of 5 signatures (private keys) to be used to unlock a wallet / send tokens from an address.

Using a multi sig wallet, you could, for example have one key that you can give your wife and another you give to another trusted person. That way, tokens could only be removed from the wallet if two out of the three parties agreed and provided their private keys.

Once again, multi sig wallets can be a blessing or a curse. In a 2/3 multi-sig wallet, you have added protection, because if one of the private keys is lost, you can still access the wallet, however if two of the keys are lost, or if all three parties cannot agree, the tokens in the wallet will be un-spendable.

Multi-sig wallets may be a great solution to prevent your private keys from being lost or your money taken from your wallet by a thief or hacker without your consent.

Corporations will tend to use multi-signature wallets more often than individuals because they work with much larger amounts of money / tokens.

Remember: there is no best way to manage your private keys – it's up to you to determine best practices for your crypto holdings.

Before we leave the topic of wallets and private key management, we have to talk about Hot Wallets.

Hot Wallets

Some wallets and all exchanges use what are called hot wallets – this means that the exchange or the wallet provider is the keeper of your private keys, NOT you.

Why would anyone allow an exchange or wallet to do this? Convenience. If you trust the wallet or the exchange where you have put your crypto tokens, a hot wallet relieves you of the burden of managing your private key(s).

This is like having a bank account with a major financial institution. The bank has access to your accounts, and can freeze or withdraw the money if they so choose.

The bank can close your account for 'suspicious activity' or in response to a court order. Yes, you have the convenience of an easy-to-use account, but the risks may outweigh the benefits – it's up to you.

In bank accounts, just like hot wallets, you also bear the risk of the wallet being hacked. If a wallet or an exchange has millions of tokens or millions of dollars of fiat currency under its control, it becomes a honeypot for hackers, thieves, governments, law enforcement and taxing authorities.

Unfortunately, to use exchanges, and in order to use certain technologies or participate in the modern banking system, you, the customer, must bear all these risks – that's why Bitcoin was invented as a peer-to-peer, decentralized store of value.

Exchanges

Exchanges are marketplaces where buyers and sellers of crypto tokens are matched, and millions of dollars of tokens are exchanged daily. Unlike hoping to buy or sell Bitcoin to people in your local neighborhood, exchanges are highly liquid, internet-based marketplaces where multiple transactions can occur in seconds, amongst tens of thousands of buyers and sellers.

Large exchanges, such as Poloniex, Bittrex, HitBTC, and Bitfinex (there are more major exchanges in addition to these), are places where you can trade between dozens or even hundreds crypto tokens, most of which have sufficiently liquid markets.

Remember when we talked about fiat gateways and regulation? Some exchanges do not allow you to transfer in and out fiat currency – you can only send crypto tokens to the exchange to be traded or withdraw crypto tokens.

The current crypto reserve currency is Bitcoin (BTC), however other market pairs are starting to appear, such as Ethereum (ETH), Litecoin (LTC), or even Ripple (XRP). This means that often, you'll have to convert your fiat into Bitcoin or Ethereum, and then send it to an exchange.

Alternatively, let's say you have Siacoin or Neo and you want to withdraw them from an exchange – you may have to convert those tokens into Bitcoin or Ethereum, and then withdraw them.

Depending on whether a given token has an active wallet that you can download, you may or may not be able to withdraw a given token to your personally held wallet for that token.

Note: exchanges use hot wallets, so you may not want to keep your holdings on an exchange for very long. Even though some exchanges claim to keep users' funds in cold storage, exchanges are honeypots users have lost millions of dollars of tokens to hackers.

Exchange Hacks and Problems

Some noteworthy hacks have been perpetrated

against Mount Gox, Bitfinex, and other exchanges. Recently, BTC-e exchange was seized by US authorities, and thousands of users may never get their holdings back again.

Mt. Gox was run by a man named Mark Karpeles. Mt. Gox lost hundreds of thousands of Bitcoins overnight when a hacker compromised the exchange in 2013. There are still lawsuits against Mt. Gox, which was forced into bankruptcy, and is rumored to be working to repay its creditors.

The Mt. Gox hack burned a lot of people in the industry and hurt confidence in Bitcoin for a long time. It was a significant reason why Bitcoin's price, which had gone up to approximately $1,200 at the time, ended up falling dramatically over several months to $200.

We now know that Bitcoin and other cryptocurrencies have since recovered and then some, with current prices at the time of this writing of $4,200. However, hacks like this will continue to take place and act as stumbling blocks to widespread adoption of crypto tokens.

There have been several other notable exchange

problems that you should be aware of: In early 2017, Chinese exchanges suddenly halted withdrawals, ultimately trapping people's money on their exchanges.

This year, BitFinex exchange suffered a hack where they halted fiat withdrawals, only allowing people to withdraw cryptocurrency.

Poloniex suffered DDOS (Distributed Denial of Service) attacks for at least a week. This caused people to panic and try to withdraw money from the exchange which they couldn't do immediately. Many people couldn't even log into their accounts for days.

Even mundane problems, such as too many new account holders, strained Poloniex's support ticket system, causing delays of 30-90 days in answering tickets.

Exchanges and Regulatory Compliance

Exchanges have to comply with AML / KYC regulations, and will ask for escalating levels of identification an verification to use their service, and to withdraw your tokens. For example, with a low level of verification, you may be restricted from withdrawing your money from an exchange entirely, or restricted to withdrawing $2,000 USD a day. You may be barred from margin trading, market orders, or other activity reserved for more highly verified accounts.

Hodlers & Crypto Traders

There are many crypto enthusiasts who believe the long-term values of various tokens will be many times higher than they are now. Just in the past year, for instance, Bitcoin rose from $600 to $4,200, Ethereum rose from $7 to nearly $400, Dash rose from $11 to $300, and other tokens have appreciated 20x to 100x.

Hodlers

Hodlers (a misspelling of holders) are crypto enthusiasts who buy and hold crypto tokens long term, with the expectation of long term gain.

Crypto Traders

Traders, who have the opposite behavior of hodlers, don't merely buy or sell their crypto one time – a large subset of exchange users are active traders, for instance. Just like with stocks, bonds, futures, and other assets, cryptocurrency trading is growing fast.

Some people day trade, while others will swing trade and use what's called technical analysis, meaning they will look at the up and down movements of a given crypto token and trade based on that information on an hourly daily, weekly, or monthly basis. Exchanges and traders resemble the equities and futures markets on a much smaller scale.

With the rise of artificial intelligence and machine learning, there are now automated trading bots that will trade for you such as Haasbot, C.A.T. Bot (Cryptocurrency Automatic Trader) and Zenbot.

These AI Bots work with the API of various exchanges to trade algorithmically, scalping profits from high speed buying and selling of various tokens on an exchange, as well as arbitraging across various exchanges. Users pay fees to use these bots that trade cryptocurrencies on their behalf.

Although AI trading bots are a relatively new phenomenon, they are starting to show up in most exchanges, and can dramatically affect the markets for various tokens.

In 2017, because of trading bots executing algorithmically and automatically, the GDAX exchange suffered a flash crash of Ethereum (ETH crashing from $300 down to $0.40 in a matter of minutes) when a multimillion dollar sell order forced margin calls on many accounts and triggered stop loss sell orders.

Still Other Ways to Obtain Crypto Tokens (LocalBitcoins.com)

Localbitcoins.com is meant for local purchases and sales of Bitcoin and other crypto tokens, often face-to-face, in person transactions. Because there is very little AML/KYC verification to open an account, the site is attractive for many libertarians and crypto anarchists.

Once your account is funded and live, you can post an ad to offer to buy or offer to sell crypto to people in your local area. You can also respond to an ad for someone who wants to buy or sell. Site users have a ratings system, which can help give you an idea of a seller or buyer's history and help you feel comfortable in dealing with a stranger.

Many localbitcoins.com transactions happen in person; traders will meet at a nearby Starbucks, Denny's, or other communal location (depends on the country you live in) or at a bank.

Some transactions don't require face to face activity – buyers can deposit fiat into a seller's bank account, show their receipt / proof of deposit, and then have Bitcoin transferred into their wallet.

Although there may be a lot of activity in your area, and buying Bitcoin this way is more anonymous than other ways, you have to be careful. There have been several local bitcoin traders that trade for a living, i.e. doing it "commercially", who have been arrested because they didn't have a money transmitter's license, and didn't have AML / KYC policies for customers.

There is a de-minimus exemption, at least in the United States, that appears to be below $3,000 USD transaction size, but you have to be careful. You may be somewhat protected if you buy through websites such as LocalBitcoins.com, however it may be safer to buy from online exchanges that send to be more regulated.

Note: I am not providing legal, tax, investment, or any other advice. You should consult with the proper professionals should you decide to transact.

One example of a bitcoin trader who did run into legal trouble is Morpheus Titania, a former window shield repair guy and consummate salesman, who claims he was living exclusively using bitcoin, and on rare occasion, cash. I had the chance to interview him before he was arrested in April of 2017, presumably due to this LocalBitcoins.com trades (which apparently were numerous).

As of the writing of this book, Morpheus was first charged with possessing ammunition as a previously convicted felon, however, it appears that the real reason he was arrested (pure speculation on my part) is because he was a prolific local bitcoin trader who may have crossed into the realm of needing to be licensed as a money transmitter and conducing AML / KYC compliance on customers.

From what I knew, Morpheus was trading only for his personal use, and didn't intend to act as a bonified money transmitter, however that's for the court system to decide. He was incarcerated for several months with no bail available to him, so you can see that the local trading of cryptocurrencies can carry severe penalties and jail time if you aren't careful and limit the scope of your trades.

ShapeShift.io

I had the opportunity to interview Erik Voorhees, CEO of Shapeshift, and a prominent figure in the crypto world. Shapeshift's platform supports approximately 50+ tokens, and allows people to exchange their token for other tokens.

For example, if you want to convert your Dash into Ethereum, you can Shapeshift it using the website or app. You can move back and forth between combinations of 50+ different crypto tokens using their service, and shapeshift, because it is not a custodian of your money at any time, does not require AML / KYC compliance and does not require not ALLOW users to have accounts.

You simply designate the send and receive addresses for your tokens, and the originating crypto token and the final token you want to shapeshift to, and voila! Within minutes, and with minimal fees, you can change one cryptocurrency for another.

One important thing to note, is that the amount of each tokens that can be exchanged is limited to relatively modest amounts. This is because Shapeshift, to keep fees as low as possible, and to minimize trade times, price slippage, and Shapeshift's risk, limits the size of token exchanges.

When doing these transactions, Shapeshift is acting as the buyer for your crypto (using their own money), and then selling a different crypto token back to the user from its own holdings. Shapeshift allows users to seamlessly change from currency to token to token.

Another interesting point to note is Shapeshift's integration with wallets such as Jaxx, for example. There's a Shapeshift icon right within the Jaxx wallet and Shapeshift is integrating with more and more platforms as time goes by.

Their interface is simple to use, and they don't collect customer data, which is appealing to many crypto enthusiasts and privacy advocates. Shapeshift doesn't accept any fiat; only bitcoin or other cryptocurrencies.

There are still more ways to buy, sell, hodl, trade, and exchange blockchain tokens, however this chapter was not meant to be an exhaustive list.

CHAPTER 4

ANONYMITY, REGULATION, CRIME & TERRORISM

Anonymous vs. Pseudonymous – Is Bitcoin Anonymous?

Bitcoin was thought to be an anonymous way of moving and storing money, but unfortunately that's far from true... because bitcoin is only **pseudonymous**, (pseudo anonymous) meaning there is only some degree of anonymity.

There are now tracking services, blockchain explorers, and analytics services that can often determine who controls a given Bitcoin address, where your Bitcoin came from and was sent to, where you were geographically when you sent or received it, and where you bought it from and sold it to.

Legend has it that various exchanges such as Coinbase, Poloniex, and others can and do track crypto transactions "five hops out", meaning that these services can trace who sold you Bitcoin, who you sold Bitcoin to, and whether your Bitcoin passed through the hands of bad actors (i.e. the dark web, porn or gambling websites, or worse).

These companies have been known to shut down users' accounts if they believed that their users were involved in transferring money to, or receiving money from, bad actors, or in some cases, competing exchanges.

Don't think for a moment that these companies would also successfully fight a subpoena or other court order from a nation state to release your records. If a company was told to either cough up its users' data or be shut down, or its owners prosecuted criminally, you can bet that that company will be compelled into releasing all its information to authorities.

Are there ways to keep yourself anonymous when using Bitcoin? Perhaps, but it's extremely tricky to do so, and likely not worth it for most folks. One possible way to mask where your Bitcoin goes and where it comes from is to use a tumbler – a service that "mixes" your Bitcoin with other user transactions, and because Bitcoin is fungible, what comes out the other side of a tumbler can't truly be called "YOUR Bitcoin" vs. some other guys Bitcoin.

Yes, there are other cryptocurrencies that are trying to allow for truly anonymous transactions and holdings such as Monero, Zcash and Dash (previously called Dark Coin).

The problem is, it's incredibly difficult to be truly anonymous anymore, and these other tokens may come under more scrutiny, attack, and pressure to reveal their customers' data or shut down and be prosecuted. I think they're going to have difficulty scaling and becoming widely adopted without compromising some of their anonymity.

Regulation vs. the Free Market

Bitcoin was initially conceived to be kind of a niche product for libertarians and people who wanted to transact in peace and away from government control and authority.

Unfortunately, my opinion is that, for bitcoin to scale and to be used around the world, it's going to have to get closer to how traditional currencies operate.

Bitcoin's going to have to be regulated and fall under the authority of various nation-states. Hopefully it will retain its best qualities (as listed previously) and will not be under the control of a single entity or nation, but the world will have to see.

Unless Bitcoin starts to "taste like chicken" and become familiar to regular folks and is perceived as stable (not volatile), and safe and legal to use and hold, it's going to have a hard time achieving widespread use.

Large financial institutions and governments are in control and are unlikely to use Bitcoin in its current form without consumer protections, regulations, and control.

How much regulation is too much? Should we worry about overreaching regulation? Definitely – the common stance, unfortunately, is to parrot the idiocy of saying: "Well if you have nothing to hide, you have nothing to worry about."

The day may come when the powers that be decide

that you and your actions are, punishable by a large fine, imprisonment, or sanction. Ignoring the insatiable thirst of regulation by assuming that everything will work out fine is a big mistake.

We must be vigilant about SENSIBLY regulating bitcoin and other blockchain assets, not burying our heads in the sand, otherwise this new, world-changing technology may be legislated out of existence.

I would love to see a world where I can buy a coffee, pay my mortgage, and send money freely to anyone in the world with Bitcoin, but it's going to take time, change and some regulation for that to happen. Bitcoin's a completely different animal than any other money we've ever seen.

I Heard Bitcoin Is Used By Criminals & Terrorists – Shedding the Dark Past of The Silk Road

The Silk Road was a dark web marketplace where anyone could buy or sell thousands of types of illegal and prescription drugs, buy or sell weapons, malicious software, and worse. The alleged mastermind behind it, Ross Ulbricht, is now in prison for multiple life sentences. On the Silk Road, transactions were conducted exclusively in Bitcoin, which was a blessing and a curse for the cryptocurrency.

On one hand, the Silk Road helped rapidly expand the use of Bitcoin, but on the other hand, it gave it a shady past that is taking time to slough off. Even today, in 2017, a recent, worldwide ransomware attack demanded victims pay in Bitcoin.

The US government made an example of the Silk Road and of Ross Ulbricht, but the sad thing is that at the same time they were doing that, other dark web marketplaces that sold similar items sprouted up in its place and they appear to be unstoppable – like the mythical hydra monster, you chop off one head and two others sprout.

Is Bitcoin solely the domain of criminals and terrorists? Not at all. Often the first adopters of any new technology (Bitcoin is a technology) are related to less socially favored industries such as porn, or black-market industries such as illegal drugs, weapons, and sadly, worse.

Yes, criminals and terrorists often have a stake in new technologies but situations rarely stay that way. People will always use technology for both good and evil things whether it involves ransomware, child pornography, you name it.

Guess what? Cash has been and is currently used for tremendous good and for evil. So are VISA, Mastercard, bank wires, ACH deposits, barter, Paypal, stocks, bonds, futures, cryptocurrencies like Dogecoin, Dash, Monero, Zcash, Bitcoin, and every other currency, store of value, or unit of account out there.

You can't name a currency or financial instrument that HASN'T been involved in crime and/or terrorism in some way, although crime and terrorism are, at most, a minor fraction of all commerce. Most commerce is conducted by and between honest people who are simply trying to make a living and live their lives.

Nearly all currencies and technologies, while used for both good and evil, are mostly used for good and rarely for evil. In fact, bitcoin has become mostly mainstream and used for honest purposes – money transmission, remittances, buying and selling goods, and more. It must not and should not be regulated out of existence.

Bitcoin is rapidly merging with the "real world" - the traditional world of banking and finance. As it does, it's overcoming its past and shedding those bad associations. It's becoming more regulated, mainstream, and welcomed. Thank goodness.

Who Is Satoshi Nakamoto, The Creator of Bitcoin?

Bitcoin was created by a person or group, that used the name 'Satoshi Nakamoto'. No one knows if it's a male or female or if it's a single, brilliant person or 20 people. No one has ever seen him in person. No one has ever talked to him on the phone. However, several people have emailed back and forth with Satoshi, until his disappearance in 2011. Since Satoshi Nakamoto sounds like a Japanese male, I'm going to refer to him as "he".

Over the years the news media has tried to find out who Satoshi is. They once tracked down a guy named Dorian Satoshi Nakamoto and everyone harassed him, convinced he was Satoshi Nakamoto. The "real" Satoshi then sent out a public notice saying Dorian Nakamoto was not, in fact, the creator of bitcoin. Other than that, however, he hasn't answered other people claiming that they are him.

In January 2009, Satoshi released a white paper describing a new digital currency that purported to solve several existing limitations that stopped previous digital currency endeavors. When Satoshi started Bitcoin, its worth was somewhere near a tenth of a cent and back then it was easy to mine Bitcoin with a home computer.

Back in late 2010, 2011, and 2012, people could have (and did) mine 1,000, 10,000 or more bitcoins on their home computer. Some lost them and years later dug through their town dump or storage locker, looking for their lost computer. Others are still holding thousands or tens of thousands of Bitcoins they mined back in the day, and are now Bitcoin millionaires!

According to Wikipedia, Satoshi's Bitcoin holdings are worth approximately 5 billion USD as of September 2017. His Bitcoin addresses are watched closely by the bitcoin community to see if there is ever any movement of bitcoin in or out. Except for a transfer of a percentage of his wealth out of his addresses many years ago, there has been no activity, only adding to the mystery.

Why, if Satoshi is alive and supposedly has all this Bitcoin, is so much money sitting there, unused? Maybe he's afraid to move it. Maybe he lost the private keys or is dead.

If the real Satoshi ever came out, would he be arrested by a government and charged with all sorts of financial crimes? It's not only possible, but highly likely.

When Craig Wright, an Australian computer scientist and businessman, man claimed to be Satoshi several years ago, authorities hinted at arresting him for terrorism and enabling criminal activities because people have used Bitcoin to buy drugs and commit other crimes. Ridiculous, because Satoshi didn't enable anything like this – he created Bitcoin.

Before Satoshi disappeared, he gave the ability to alter bitcoin's core code to Gavin Andreesen. Subsequently, Gavin relinquished his ability to alter the code, to a group of developers called Bitcoin Core.

To date, Satoshi remains a mystery that may never be solved. The bottom line is that whoever he is, Satoshi gave the world this gift called Bitcoin. His creation has turned into an amazing technology with hundreds of thousands of people involved – a world-wide game changer. Thank you, Satoshi!

CHAPTER 5:
BLOCKCHAIN ASSET REGULATION AND COMPLIANCE

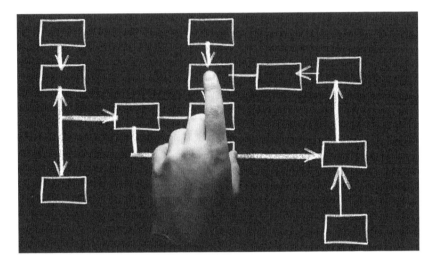

Although ~5 million people worldwide are familiar with and transact in crypto tokens, that represents less than 0.07% of the world's population. What's the chance that every government in the world is aware of blockchain and is seeking to govern, regulate, and control it? There's a **100% chance.**

Because this book focuses primarily on the United States of America, that laws and regulations that I will be discussing apply mostly to the USA. Your country may have radically different laws, acceptance, and regulation, whether stricter or more permissive than the USA.

Whether you're an individual investor, hodler, trader, occasional buyer and seller, developer, or company operating in this space, it's vital to be aware of the current and fast-changing regulatory environment.

Crypto and the 'real world' are rapidly merging, and regulation is here – more is coming. Err on the side of caution so you don't end up with tax or legal issues – or end up in jail.

Please remember that all material in this chapter is the opinion of the author, and not of the publisher or anyone else involved in the production, publishing, or dissemination of this book. I am not a CPA, nor a financial advisor, nor an attorney.

The Internal Revenue Service (IRS)

At the time of this writing, the Internal Revenue Service (IRS) considers bitcoin and other blockchain tokens to be property, not currency. Unfortunately, unlike real property (i.e. a house), you can't depreciate your crypto holdings, but you CAN hold your tokens for a year and a day and qualify for the long-term capital gains tax rate, which may be far lower than earned income.

Let's say you purchased 2 BTC on February 1st, 2017 for $1,100 per BTC, and end up selling your 2 BTC on February 5th, 2018, for $5,200 per BTC, giving you a $8,200 profit. Your gain would be taxable at the long term capital gains rate (not the entire value of the $10,400 worth of BTC you sold – just the difference in value).

A tax tactic that may be helpful, depending on your unique situation, is to sell certain tokens you own at the end of a tax year, to take losses and offset any gains you've realized. You may have to wait 30 days to buy back your tokens to not have the loss be considered a 'wash sale', however.

Let's say you bought and sold 2 BTC as in the example above, netting $8,200 profit. Let's say you also own XYZ Coin, and you sell all your XYZ coin at a $3,200 loss. You may be able to offset the two, and show a $5,000 profit ($8,200 - $3,200) instead of an $8,200 profit at the end of the tax year.

You then wait 30 days, still believing that XYZ Coin is a good long-term hold, and buy back in. Your new basis in XYZ is the new price you bought it at, not the old price you bought it at (remember this) and any gains you make on XYZ coin will be taxed.

Don't be fooled into thinking that your Bitcoin or other holdings are anonymous, have run through a tumbler, were accessed through Tor Browser, or that since you only buy locally, you're not subject to scrutiny by the IRS.

The IRS, as well as state and other taxing authorities, are fast getting up to speed on crypto tokens, and will be on the lookout to generate tax revenues from people who transact in crypto.

In your country, if you live outside the United States, be aware of the possible tax consequences as well.

How interested in blockchain is the IRS? Well, you may or may not be aware, but one of the largest US-based exchanges, Coinbase, was served by a massive subpoena by the IRS, demanding that Coinbase hand over records of all transactions of all its customers from 2013 through 2015.

This was an unprecedented action by the IRS, who suspects that some Coinbase customers may have under-reported or failed to report their crypto holdings and profits / losses.

If you fail to report or under-report your crypto holdings and transactions, you may be audited (often years after the fact), and you do NOT want to have tax trouble, which tends to strike at the worst possible time.

Individual Traders & Record-Keeping

Record keeping can become a huge chore, especially if you trade often, and transact in multiple tokens. Some people only have bitcoin and choose to just hold it. Others have Bitcoin, Litecoin, Dash, Monero, 5 or 6 ICOs, and 10 other tokens they're speculating in.

Active traders may make hundreds or thousands of transactions a year amongst 6 different exchanges, in and out of wallets and bank accounts, and have very complicated reporting and tracking of profit and loss to do.

If you're doing any amount of trading or have bought and sold crypto, you need to keep records of what you bought, for what price, how much you bought, when you bought (date), and all that same information when you sell.

Luckily there is software out there to assist people in record keeping – ask your accountant or tax advisor for software that may help you track all your transactions.

Anti-Money Laundering (AML) and Know-Your-Customer (KYC) Regulations

Bitcoin and other crypto tokens act and are transacted on a global scale. You also must be aware of anti-money laundering (AML) and Know Your Customer (KYC) requirements. Although these requirements may differ slightly from country to country, these regulations are present in some form or another in every country on earth.

Many people interested in crypto tokens get annoyed at what they perceive to be unreasonable, required levels of documentation to open an account at an exchange, or to buy or sell crypto tokens using fiat currency.

Just like a bank account, when you're trying to open an account at an exchange or use a Bitcoin ATM, you may be asked to show a copy of your driver's license, or show a video of yourself holding your passport, or to submit other documents to verify your identity.

If you want to move larger amounts of cryptocurrency, to trade on margin, or withdraw large amount of crypto from your account, elevated levels of identity verification and vetting will be required for you to have the access you're looking for...

...but why?

AML / KYC requirements, that's why. Banks and other financial institutions are heavily regulated by their governments, and increasingly, so are companies that act as custodians of your crypto tokens or companies that act as money transmitters.

If a company fails to have a strong AML / KYC policy, they risk being shut down, having all funds seized or worse, jail or prison for the company executives and employees. This is especially the case when companies move tokens / money across borders – state or national borders.

Companies are not trying to invade your privacy for fun – they are required to vet and verify who is using their platform, causing them to act as a custodian of your money, or who is transmitting tokens and money through their channels.

If you own a company in the crypto space, realize that there is support and assistance out there to guide you to be compliant with state and federal laws (in the United States). Undoubtedly, there are legal, tax, business, and financial consultants in other countries as well.

For example, I interviewed Joseph Ciccolo, founder of Bit AML (www.BitAML.com) – a company that helps businesses create compliant AML / KYC policies.

In the interview, Joe Ciccolo stated that he believes most companies want to comply and are actively trying to comply - they may simply be unaware of how to do so.

Keep in mind that AML / KYC compliance issues not only apply to businesses but may also apply to local bitcoin traders (individuals).

You may have seen in the news, that several active, local bitcoin traders that have been arrested and prosecuted for being unlicensed money transmitters. This reinforces how very important it is for anyone, no matter on how small a scale, to make sure that you are complaint with AML/KYC regulations and perhaps to be aware of what constitutes 'money transmission' on a commercial scale in your state or country.

Securities Laws (the SEC & FINRA)

In the United States, different agencies consider cryptocurrency and bitcoin to be different things. As mentioned earlier, the IRS currently considers it to be property. The U.S. Securities and Exchange Commission (SEC), the Financial Industry Regulatory Authority (FINRA) and other financial organizations may now consider certain blockchain assets to be securities and subject to regulation and registration as securities.

At the time of this writing, ICOs (Initial Coin Offerings) are at a fever pitch and are being issued on a daily basis. WATCH OUT, because as an issuer of a token, you may have to register your token as a security.

Even the name 'ICO' is problematic, because it may lead investors to believe that what they are investing in is an IPO (initial public offering of a stock), merely under a slightly different name.

Some companies are requiring that investors submit documentation to prove that they are an accredited investor to even participate in an ICO. Many companies are leaving the United States, believing that, by issuing an ICO in a different country, they are safe from United States regulations.

Companies that issue tokens (and several exchanges) have even taken the drastic step of blocking residents of the United States from participating in their ICO or doing business with people in the USA.

Regulation is coming and it's coming quickly. The ICO space is about to get ugly for some of the companies that issued tokens on the advice of their attorneys (or without that advice) – tokens that resembled securities – tokens that fail the 'Howie test'.

Are You A Money Transmitter?

If you are buying and selling crypto tokens, there's a vast difference between you doing it for your own personal use vs. commercial purpose. Where's the dividing line? That depends on the state you live in, and that state's laws. If you transact with customers outside of your state, then you must be aware of the laws in that particular state as well.

There are a number of local bitcoins traders and people that thought they were small fish in a big pond that have been arrested for failing to operate with a money transmitter's license.

If you're trading bitcoins and other cryptocurrencies on any scale with other people, even locally, be aware that you may be required to be licensed as a money transmitter depending on your state and your country, or licensed in some other way in order to conduct business.

The size of your transactions, the velocity and number of your transactions, and local regulations all play a part in how you may or may not be subject to scrutiny and regulation – be aware and be cautious. If you are moving crypto internationally you're very likely to be unaware of another country's laws.

Additionally, in the United States if you're going to buy and sell crypto across state lines you may need a money transmitter's license in your state, and a license in every other state you trade with.

Let's say you're a prolific crypto trader and you trade with people in six different states. If you get caught as an unlicensed money transmitter you may be hit with charges in each of the six states for being an unlicensed money transmitter, for failing to have an AML / KYC policy, and more.

In April 2017, a local bitcoin trader in Arizona who goes under the moniker 'Morpheus Titania' was arrested by multiple state and federal agencies. The scope of his arrest and the attention from various agencies was unbelievable - they acted as if he was the world's biggest criminal.

I don't know the full extent of Morpheus' activities, but he seemed to be a regular guy - a local bitcoins trader in Arizona who was trading to make money to live - not as a business. Now look what happened - he was arrested, denied bail (!?!?@?!) and has been in jail for months, awaiting trial.

He wasn't even initially charged with operating an unlicensed money transmitter business. This is just one example of many of how serious this business can be. When it comes to money and now to crypto, this is serious business and it's being treated as such by all governments around the world.

Why Understanding, Complying With, and Having Legal Counsel Is Super Important

As crypto and blockchain applications grow, there are professionals training themselves to be tax, AML / KYC, money transmission, securities law, legal experts because there will be lawsuits, criminal complaints, tax implications, securities implications, and contract law implications of blockchain assets and blockchain use cases.

You definitely need legal, tax, and financial counsel if you want to operate a business in this world, especially anything having to do with Bitcoin or other crypto tokens.

A few of the professionals who are well-versed and focused on providing advice in the blockchain space are Patrick Murck and Marco Santorini of Cooley LLP as well as Daniel Winters (CPA), who are referenced herein.

Just like the internet was the wild west 25 year ago, it has rapidly merged with the real world and with real world regulation. This same thing is happening with the world of crypto.

Many entrepreneurs in this space act first, then seek forgiveness later. That thinking might have worked until recently, but as court cases start to pop up, as law and regulations come into place, there is going to be a precedent and a track record set.

Any company or individual that says, "I didn't know", or "I'm sorry please forgive my company's conduct", may not be spared harsh punishment.

Ignorance of the law is no excuse, as the powers that be, claim. You had better believe that the crypto and blockchain worlds are very quickly merging with the "real world" as well and that means laws and regulations WILL be applied by governments, tax authorities, and regulators worldwide.

For example, look at Amazon. All 50 states in the United States have been in and out of court with Amazon and other online businesses, demanding that Amazon be required to pay sales tax if they ship to their state. Think about it - if gigantic, well-funded companies like Amazon spend tens of millions to fight regulation, you know that it's going to become an issue for the small guys.

Chapter 6:
Mining, Nodes & Governance Models

How Mining Works

The name, "Bitcoin miner" is a misnomer. Miners aren't digging for physical Bitcoins using picks and shovels, but are instead competing to solve a math puzzle, where the reward for doing so is a certain amount of Bitcoin (currently 12.5 BTC), created by the software protocol and "credited to the address" of the winning miner.

Miners assemble transactions that occur on the Bitcoin network into groups called 'blocks of transactions. A miner that wins a given 10-minute-long math puzzle, earns the right to record the block of transactions they assembled onto the Bitcoin blockchain, triggering the Bitcoin protocol award. The miner is also awarded the transaction fees associated with the transactions in their block (the block reward).

The act of putting in mathematical computing power (i.e. electricity to run computers) is called work, and the winner of the mining contest has shown sufficient "proof of work" to win the puzzle, and is rewarded for their efforts.

To recap, whoever wins the puzzle receives two things: 1) The fees for the transactions in the block that they won the right to add. Those fees right now account for approx. 10% of the total block reward; 2) The other 90% of the reward is receipt of new bitcoins that are created by the bitcoin protocol system (currently 12.5 bitcoins) every 10 minutes, 24 hours a day, 7 days a week, 365 days a year, a new math contest is begun by the Bitcoin protocol.

Bitcoin's Block Reward & The 'Halvening'

Bitcoin's protocol is set so that every four years the block reward is cut in half. In approximately the year 2140, the block reward will be reduced to zero because all of the bitcoins that could be mined, or created, will have been.

Right now, there is a maximum limit right 21 million Bitcoins that can be created. That may not sound like much, especially if you hope that Bitcoin becomes a true world currency can process thousands of transactions second, but remember: bitcoin is divisible to eight decimals places (1 satoshi = 0.00000001 BTC).

Twenty-one million multiplied by 100 million is a HUGE number, so there's plenty of room for Bitcoin's price to grow, even to $1,000,000 per Bitcoin. 1 Million divided by 100 million is 0.01 – the equivalent of expressing $1 dollar and 1 cent.

Can You Mine Bitcoin at Home?

Individuals used to be able to use their laptop's CPU to mine for Bitcoin. Then people discovered graphics cards could mine hundreds or thousands of times faster than CPUs and switched to using graphics cards. This made all of the CPUs that were mining unable to compete.

Companies then started designing and using ASIC

(application specific integrated circuit) computers to mine, which were thousands of times faster than graphics cards, or FPGAs (field programmable gate arrays). ASICs were specifically designed to run Bitcoin protocol mining calculations and nothing else.

As late as 2014, individuals still had a hope of being able to competitively mine Bitcoin using their laptop, and/or graphics card.

Today, with the advent of ASIC chips that can process trillions of math calculations per second, and rooms full of hundreds or thousands of ASIC computers crunching away, there's little hope for small scale operations or individuals to effectively mine Bitcoin (there is still the ability to competitively mine other blockchain tokens, however).

In addition to expensive, noisy, heat-producing, power-hungry computers required to mine Bitcoin, electricity costs in many countries make Bitcoin mining unprofitable on a small scale.

In 2017, the mining game has become ultra-competitive and technology heavy. Companies such as

Bitmain have invested millions of dollars in the latest integrated circuit fabrication techniques to make super-fast, multi tera-hash (tera-hash = 1 trillion calculations per second) mining computers.

Not to be outdone, Nvidia has created a line of graphics cards specifically tuned to mine Ethereum and other crypto tokens at a super-fast rate. World supplies of graphics cards and Bitcoin miners can't compete with miners' interests, and shortages are common.

Who Mines Bitcoin Commercially?

Who are the companies, individuals, or groups of miners, located all over the world, who compete to solve Bitcoin's math problem every 10 minutes?

Bitcoin mining operations exist all over the world – China, Iceland, North and South America – everywhere. This makes Bitcoin mining decentralized and resistant to attack or co-option by a single nation-state or group of wealthy individuals, because there is global competition to earn the right to update the network and to profit handsomely from it.

Today's competitive mining operations may only have 2 or 5% of the total network's computing (hash) power, yet require hundreds or even thousands of ASIC miners to achieve that level of market share.

Hash power is the mathematical 'juice' or number of mathematical operations that a given computer or network of computers uses to work on a given math problem. As of this writing, the total global hashrate for Bitcoin is approximately 7.5 Exahashes per second (7.5 x $10 \wedge 18$ hashes per second!)

What Mining Operations Look Like

What do mining operations look like? You'd probably be very disappointed to find out. Mining operations look very similar to big datacenters – rooms full of racks of identical-looking computers, merrily buzzing away, producing tremendous heat and tremendous electricity bills.

If you were to visit most mining facilitates, you would probably see a rundown warehouse on the outside – You'd never know what was happening on the inside, as mining companies are usually hidden from public view and certainly don't have storefronts.

In many cases, miners are afraid of being robbed, arrested, killed, extorted, or compromised or co-opted by powerful interests. Mining can be a nasty business.

That's why, typically miners are very secretive about their operations. In some countries where miners operate, if discovered by government (ex: Venezuela), miners could be and have been arrested and prosecuted.

Mining operations run on power from burning coal, from a hydroelectric dam, geothermal, wind, solar, or other major power source. They are trying to use cheap sources of electricity to run their computers to ensure their mining operation is profitable. The whole Bitcoin ecosystem is rumored to consume over $1 million of electricity a day!

This electricity burn secures the Bitcoin network cryptographically through the proof of work system. This enormous hurdle to being able to update Bitcoin's blockchain is so secure that Bitcoin has yet, in its 7+ years of existence, to break down, become unusable or be hacked.

Some people say the amount of electricity used for the proof of work mining protocol is environmentally irresponsible and wasteful. Others say it is not and it is necessary for true security. Either way, this is the reality.

More Miners = Higher Mining Difficulty

An interesting facet of bitcoin mining is how the difficulty of winning the block reward adjusts based on the amount of total hashrate used to find the block reward. As more companies mine and use faster computers and more of them, the difficulty of the ten-minute race to win the block reward increases.

That's why the current hash rate is so unbelievably high at 7.5 exahashes – Bitcoin mining is profitable and becoming more competitive every day. The block reward math problem is currently SO difficult, it takes computers making 7.5×10^{18} guesses per second for 10 minutes to solve!

Mining Operations and Hash Power

Some of the largest mining operations use hundreds to thousands of their own computers as well as run mining pools to further bolster their total hash rate.

Some of the largest mining pools as of this writing are shown in the chart below:

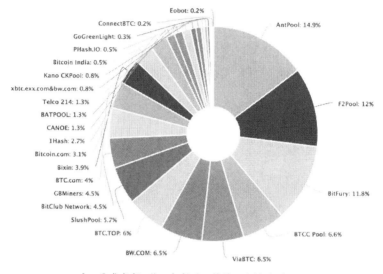

Image Credited to https://www.buybitcoinworldwide.com/mining/pools

This chart also hints at where mining tends to concentrate geographically, including countries or regions that have the cheap electricity or cheap / renewable energy (geothermal, solar, wind). Mining operations also benefit from running in cold regions (such as Iceland), due to the need to exhaust tremendous heat produced by mining computers).

There is a fear that mining cold end up being

111

centralized or concentrated in a single country; China for example. China does manufacture most ASIC equipment and also has cheap electricity, so the fear is that the government could come in and take over a large percent of the total hashrate whenever it wants.

Cloud Mining

So, what do you do if you're an individual with a laptop, but no access to cheap electricity or hundreds of ASIC computers? Cloud mining is offered by several mining operations where you 'buy hash rate' from a provider, who will spin up one or more of their mining computers (ASIC, GPU or otherwise), mine on your behalf, and offer you a share of the profits.

You'd have to consider this: why would a mining operation do this if their own mining is profitable? Several reasons come to mind:

1. Cloud mining may allow an operation to spread its capital and expense risk by having hundreds of users subsidize their costs. Because of that benefit to the mining company, they would be willing to share in their profits;

2. To squeeze out more profit, a cloud mining company could offer a reduced payout percentage to its customers, using the valid excuses that overseeing accounts, and managing hashrate for others requires the mining company to have a facility, spend electricity, pay employees, and other overhead costs.

The problem I see with cloud mining is that you don't truly know what's going on in the mining facility. You don't know if they're cheating you or not or if they did, in fact, win a given block reward.

What's to stop a mining company from claiming that they didn't mine as many blocks as they actually mined? It's up to you, the reader, but the apparent convenience of having someone else mine for you and you enjoying all the profits might not be a good a deal as it seems. However, there are some reputable companies out there.

One company that I interviewed in this space is called Genesis Mining. In addition to Bitcoin, you can mine Ethereum, Litecoin, Bitcoin Cash, Zcash and other cryptocurrencies through their service. Once you mine a given token, you could always exchange it for bitcoin, or hodl and keep your mining proceeds in their native coin.

Mining Pools

Because winning the Bitcoin block reward takes such tremendous hash rate, some people have created mining pools. For example, let's say I have two ASIC miners, you have three and Susan has seven.

We decide to pool together and combine our hash power with the goal of winning more block rewards than any of us could win on their own. This is called a mining pool, and there are many you can join.

Bitcoin.com has a mining pool, as well as many other companies. Unlike cloud mining, to join a pool, you must have some level of computer resources and electricity to create hash rate, which you 'point' to a mining pool.

51% Attacks & Forks

Why does it matter if mining becomes centralized and a single authority or company controls a high percentage of the total network hash rate?

Because there is a way to control the Bitcoin

network, called a 51% attack. If any mining consortium has more than 51% of the hash power, they can cause the main Bitcoin blockchain to fork – i.e. split into two different chains.

According to Bitcoin protocol's rules, the longest chain (the majority blockchain) will become the preferred chain to mine, and the minority chain will be orphaned, making its transactions invalid.

A miner that controls 51% or more of the total hash rate can mine blocks according to a modified software protocol (such as mining larger blocks, or blocks with preferred transactions), even if the rest of the network does not agree with the majority miner. This would allow the majority miner to take the Bitcoin blockchain down a path of their choosing, perhaps with dramatically different parameters.

Thankfully, the current reality shows that Bitcoin mining is highly decentralized, across so many countries that it's unlikely a 51% attack would happen... Unless there was a conspiracy between several large mining pools who collude to dominate the total hash rate.

Some people theorize that a nation-state would have enough resources to take 51%+ of the total hash rate, but to date this has not happened.

Mining, just like everything else in the Crypto World, is extremely political, and subject to volatility and constant change.

Nodes

A full node is a computer that has a downloaded record of the entire blockchain for a given coin on it. Some computers only have more recent transactions on them, and are called 'light clients'.

Nodes help verify transactions, and communicate with each other about the state of a given blockchain. For instance, the Bitcoin network is rumored to have over 5,000 full nodes running worldwide, in countries all over the world.

When a miner successfully mines a block, and earns the right to add that block to the blockchain, it must communicate that block's transactions to all nodes in the Bitcoin network as quickly and accurately as possible.

Once a newly mined block is verified, then added to a node's existing ledger copy, the new, updated ledger propagates to all the nodes in the Bitcoin network, and all nodes accept and update the new ledger.

How Much Data Comprises a Bitcoin Full Node?

The Bitcoin ledger grows every 10 minutes, when it adds a new block of transactions. It is currently 100 gigabytes in size and growing.

Depending on the token / coin, how large its particular block size is, and how fast the software protocol adds new blocks (ex: Bitcoin is 10 minutes, Litecoin is 4 minutes) all blockchains grow at various rates.

Blockchains that become Terabytes, Petabytes, Exabytes or larger may become a potentially serious problem in the future. The reason for this is that computers cannot quickly download terabytes (or more) of data, and may not even be able to hold this much data. This limits which devices must run a light client and may centralize a given network, making it depend on semi-centralized full nodes.

In addition, it costs money to not only store a large amount of data, but to run a server for that data. This is why various tokens incentivize full nodes with rewards of valuable tokens (ex: Proof of Stake tokens such as Dash, Stratis, Neo, and more).

The Cost of Decentralization

The more computers and the more places around the world that keep a full copy of a given coin's blockchain, the more decentralized that coin becomes, and the harder it becomes to attack and damage, destroy, co-opt, or corrupt that coin's network.

Decentralized networks are hard to attack and to corrupt that network because there are exact copies of a given blockchain ledger worldwide, on thousands of different computers. It's like backing up your computer to 5,000 different computers around the world – good luck trying to delete all your data!

Because the data that comprises blockchains is encrypted, then cryptographically secured, (remember the Jenga Tower® analogy of how blockchains work) it's nearly impossible for anyone to destroy or corrupt this information; even a government or a nation state. Decentralization is one of the most powerful premises behind Bitcoin and other blockchain assets.

Running Your Own Full Node

Regardless of the coin, running a full node takes computer savvy, equipment, time, and knowledge. You must maintain your node and keep it active and connected to its network for it to be useful and reliable to the network, and to earn rewards from Proof of Stake tokens, such as Dash, Neo, Stratis, QTUM, and more.

If your node doesn't have at least 99% uptime, and if this happens across many nodes, it would result in an unreliable network that had frequent slowdowns, outages, and a declining user base.

For a small fee, there are individuals and companies (like Node 40, who sets up and maintains Dash master nodes) will run a full node, and do all of work and maintenance for you.

Scaling, Block Size, Block Timing & Mass Adoption

Bitcoin is one of the most heavily used networks right now, and is only able to handle about four (4) transactions a second. If it's going to scale and become a worldwide and widely-used currency, it needs to handle a lot more capacity. To compare, Visa and Mastercard handle 10,000 or more transactions per second, so we're still a long way off from achieving that level of scale.

Unfortunately, because no single actor is in control of Bitcoin, how to scale Bitcoin safely and effectively has become a raging, ongoing, politicized debate.

As user adoption grows, other tokens, such as Ethereum, are running into scaling issues as well. A protocol named "the lightning network" is in development, which will allow a large percent of Bitcoin transactions to happen 'off chain' and only be verified periodically on chain. Ethereum's current scaling solution is called "Raiden" and is being developed as of this publication.

It's ironic that bitcoin is so political because it was meant to be apolitical and away from government, however, it's probably become one of the most politicized phenomena I've ever seen. Online debates include name-calling, censorship of posts on Reddit and other websites, and public verbal attacks on various people in the space.

The Bitcoin Block Size Debate

Bitcoin's core developers are cautious and security oriented; they appear to want to make sure there's a scaling solution that works, and one that will keep the integrity and characteristics of Bitcoin, such as decentralization and peer-to-peer transfers of value.

One of the most contentious ongoing debates has been the size of the blocks that are added to the Bitcoin blockchain.

Some groups want bigger blocks, which will likely mean more transactions can be processed by the network in each 10-minute window.

Other groups do not want the block size to be increased, fearing that larger block sizes will lead to miners becoming more centralized and too powerful vs. other network stakeholders.

The current Bitcoin block size is 1 megabyte (although that has recently increased due to the adoption of a protocol enhancement called Segregated Witness 'SegWit') This means, in each 10-minute period, as many Bitcoin transactions that can fit into the block size will fit, until the block is full.

Since each block is mined every 10 minutes, the idea is, the more transactions that get stuffed into a given block, the more transactions the network can process in the given time period.

As more and more people get involved in Bitcoin, the number of transactions has been growing quickly, and the bitcoin network has been very slow at times.

To get transactions included in a block, some people are attaching higher fees to their transactions, to make them preferable to send (preferable for the miners to include in a given block).

In general, the Bitcoin network's average transaction fee has been growing very quickly, and is now at an average of $6-$8 per transaction, which makes cheap transactions impossible, due to the fees (ex: buying a $4 cup of coffee and paying $8 in fees is ridiculous)

In addition to increasing the Bitcoin block size, other scaling solutions have been proposed, such as the Lightning Network, which would move most small dollar and non-critical transactions off the blockchain.

The Lightning Network would allow for nearly instantaneous transactions, and possibly hundreds or thousands of transactions a second, which would help Bitcoin scale tremendously.

Another solution I referred to earlier is called SegWit, or Segregated Witness. SegWit takes part of each Bitcoin transaction (the digital signatures), verifies them, but excludes them from being recorded on the Bitcoin blockchain, which would free up perhaps 30% more space in a given block. Litecoin first accepted SegWit, and now Bitcoin has accepted and activated SegWit. How all of this will play out remains to be seen, as of this writing.

Proof of Stake vs. Proof of Work

Bitcoin's network uses a 'proof of work' governance / mining system. To recap, miners must show proof that they 'did the work' to solve the math puzzle required of them to earn the block and transaction rewards.

Other coins use what is called a 'proof of stake' system, where stakeholders – i.e. individuals that own and hold a certain amount of a given token, can help that network in several ways, and be compensated for doing so.

A good example of this is Dash (formerly called Dark Coin). In Dash's system, if you hold 1,000 Dash coins, you earn master node status, which gives you voting rights for proposals made by people who are working to improve the Dash network. Master node holders also must have continuous uptime, and help clear and vote on network transactions – i.e. helping to run the Dash network as a full node holder and master node.

In return for running a full node and a master node, Dash holders are compensated with an additional 1.2 Dash by the software protocol approximately every 7-8 days (as of this writing, but subject to change).

An example of how the Dash voting system can help benefit people is the case of Amanda B. Johnson, who runs a weekly YouTube video series on Dash. She reports on news and events in the Dash community, and helps to spread the adoption of Dash.

Amanda is compensated for her work, because she put in a proposal to the Dash system, which was voted on by several hundred master nodes. Since a majority of master nodes agreed to her proposal, the Dash network paid Amanda a certain amount of Dash monthly from its treasury, as compensation for her weekly videos and interviews. That's the power and flexibility of the master node system in the Dash world, and an example of the potential of a proof of stake system vs. proof of work.

Other tokens that have a proof of stake system are, Stratis, Lisk, NEO, Kore, and others. Ethereum has been considering changing from proof of work to proof of stake, but this has not yet occurred as of this writing.

CHAPTER 7:

VENTURE CAPITAL, ICOS, & OTHER STARTUP FUNDING SOURCES

It is probably no surprise that there's tremendous interest in the bitcoin blockchain currency space from individuals, institutional investors, governments, corporations, and more. A number of venture capital firms and hedge funds have now have sprung up to capitalize on the demand.

There are hundreds of companies forming, to focus on various blockchain use cases, such as securing your identity using the blockchain, getting control of your medical data, sending remittances worldwide, interbank payment channels, internet of things (IOT) and blockchain integration, and on and on.

The blockchain space is one of the hottest around (some call it internet 3.0) and it's going to continue that way for the next several years at least. Amazingly, at a combined market cap of approx. 150 billion dollars, the blockchain and crypto space is still a tiny fraction of other markets, such as real estate and equities.

Some well-known Venture Capital firms in this space are: Pantera Capital, Blockchain.capital, Digital Currency Group, Andreessen Horowitz, and Union Square Ventures.

There's a tremendous entrepreneurial spirit in the blockchain space, and by definition, when you're involved in the crypto space, you're on the bleeding edge.

Because crypto threatens to disrupt most mainstream industries, it's not easy to raise money from banks or large financial institutions, as other companies have done. That's why it can be very hard to attract traditional money.

The crypto sector relies a great deal on venture capitalists, and now, on ICOs (initial coin offerings). As of this writing, there's an explosion of ICOs – literally every week there are new ICOs happening.

How ICOs (Initial Coin Offerings) Work

An ICO is a method of fundraising whereby a nascent company issues a token to investors. Some of the tokens are issued purely to raise money to fund development of the project, and others are issued with the intention of providing users access to software, a protocol, or network.

These companies will have a presale of a certain amount of their tokens at a heavily discounted price, and then have a regular ICO where the token price continues to rise until a funding goal is reached.

For example, ABC Token decides to raise money for their blockchain-based, decentralized, peer-to-peer storage of encrypted data, which allows people to store their data in a decentralized cloud (across many computers) in an encrypted way (instead of without protection and not on a centralized server bank: like

Amazon Web Services, Google Docs, Dropbox, or iCloud).

ABC Company has a goal of raising $50 million dollars by issuing its ABC token, which gives users the ability to store their data by accessing ABCs blockchain-based software protocol. The protocol requires X amount of ABC tokens to store Y amount of data, so the token acts like a Software Access Token or Utility Token.

ABC proclaims a pre-ICO funding round of $15 million dollars, at 25 cents a token, and offers a 10% bonus to pre-ICO investors. Once the $15-million dollar goal is met, ABC will commence an ICO funding round for the remaining $35 million, at 50 cents a token for 10 days, then 75 cents a token for the next 10 days, then $1 a token for the next 10 days. (any of this sounding eerily familiar?)

Investors in the pre-ICO or ICO round are allowed to buy a certain number of tokens at the agreed-upon price, but must wait 60 days to have their tokens credited to their wallet. After that time, investors may have to wait months longer for the token to start trading on a secondary exchange, like Bittrex, Poloniex, Bitstamp, Bitfinex, etc.

The behavior of many investors has been to buy pre-ICO or ICO tokens, then dump some or all of them once the tokens hit the secondary trading market. Some tokens have lost most of their value and never recovered, others have skyrocketed in value and have never looked back at their pre-ICO or ICO prices. Some have failed completely, losing investors' money.

Because of the pump and dump nature of ICO investors, some tokens have decided to reward hodlers with a proof-of-stake model. When a coin goes ICO, its price may spike many tens or hundreds of dollars. The people that get in early will sell and cause the price to pump up and then crash. Then it takes months or a year or more in many cases, for the price to come back to any meaningful level. One year, in the world of stocks and equities, isn't considered long term. However, in the world of crypto tokens, a year is an eternity.

The Coming ICO Regulatory Crackdown

An unfortunate side effect, is that the blockchain space has attracted some unscrupulous people that have no intention of developing their projects; people who are simply scamming investors out of their money, to the tune of tens of millions of dollars.

As you can imagine, regulatory bodies around the world have become highly suspicious and concerned about the proliferation of ICOs.

In the United States, the Securities and Exchange Commission has publicly commented that many initiatives that raised money by issuing a token should have registered their opportunity as a security offering and may be subject to being shut down, to penalties, and to increased regulation.

Because of the regulatory scrutiny, many companies have fled to Zug, Switzerland, or other countries, or disallowed US-based investors to participate in ICOs, thinking this will save them from regulatory scrutiny or legal trouble.

As of this writing, however, governments around the world, including China, Russia, Israel, South Korea, the United States, Thailand, and many more have issued warnings that say they intend to regulate the ICO space and perhaps shut down some or more ICO fund raises.

China has taken, by far, the most aggressive stance against ICOs, and has recently banned all ICOs and demanded that 65+ projects return investors' money. China has also moved to shut down cryptocurrency exchanges, and is deciding how to regulate the ICO process, or continue to disallow it completely. China may also shut down crypto mining, and block use of cryptocurrencies as best it can.

Be aware that every single government around the world (no exaggeration) is well aware of blockchain, and is considering how to regulate it, how much to regulate it, or whether to try to make it illegal completely.

My prediction, for whatever it's worth, is that within a year's time, you will see some notable cases where ICOs are legally attacked, sued, shut down, and the founders punished civilly or criminally, as they are coming under pressure more and more to be regulated as potential securities.

What Do VC's Look For In A Start-up?

When deciding which startups to invest in, it's no surprise venture capitalists in this industry look for the exact same things they look for in other industries.

To start, VCs want to preserve their principle (i.e. get their money back at worst) and profit 10x, 100x or 1,000x from the deal. VCs will look for the strength of the management team as one of the primary indicators of the potential success of a venture.

If you're a single founder, it's not nearly as powerful having several co-founders and an experienced team of people and advisors. No one person has every skill; no one person is a great developer, a great programmer, great with finances, marketing, is a great leader, and so on.

Candidates most likely to get funding in these cases would be a team that is diversified. Do they have past experience and previous wins? Do they work well together personality-wise?

Several VCs I interviewed told me that investing in a company is like a marriage. You can't just invest in a company and let them run away with your money and do whatever they want. You must be there to advise because you have a large stake in the company and will likely be intimately involved with its team for 5-10 years.

A venture capitalist's goal is to help that company grow, scale, then maybe go IPO at some point or get bought out for a 50x multiple of the company's initial valuation later on. That's how venture capitalists make their money.

First and foremost, however, they want their personality and interest to jive with the founders and team of the startups they invest in, and for their startups to have a solid team that can execute on their premise and promises.

Surprisingly, the idea the founders have, in many cases, is secondary. They want to see that the companies have some traction on their own, of course, and that they are not just a pure idea. They are looking to see that the ideas can be executed.

Even in the Blockchain World, VCs Are Specialized

Before you go looking for funding, you must consider: what types of projects are the VCs interested in? Just because you're in the Blockchain space, it doesn't mean that you're going to get money from a given VC.

Let's say your application will help large financial institutions and banks reduce their back-office processing costs. How about if you are, instead, a cryptocurrency enthusiast, and you want to allow people to send remittances (send money back home) to various African countries? Would the same type of VC be interested in both types of companies? Most likely not.

Incubators

Some VC firms run what are called incubators. Not only do they invest money in companies, but they also provide technical, managerial, and financial expertise. They want to help grow their companies into mature companies with valuations of 20, 50, 100, or even 1,000 times their initial valuation.

For example, one company I interviewed, Boost VC, has what it calls tribes. They have people in each tribe working on a different blockchain initiative.

Another company, named Dutch Chain, hosts Hackathons, where they gather groups of coders / developers who program for 36 or 48 hours with the goal of creating a minimal viable product for their idea.

Getting the Attention of VCs

In addition to knocking on doors, you can get the attention of VCs and angels by participating in hackathons and other events where they are looking to find new up and coming startups. For example, a company called Distributed ID participated in and won a hackathon, which resulted in them getting funding.

I also had the opportunity to interview the founders of Monetizing Full nodes project, Michael Folkson and Nate Basanese, who participated in the Bcoin Hackathon and won. They too gained VC interest from the event. There are on-ramps everywhere for startups.

It's good to keep in mind that no matter who you are, even a college or high school student, it doesn't mean that you can't get funding for your idea.

It's worth mentioning the Blockchain Education Network (BEN) is big on promoting hackathons and helping its student population. Just like scouts who recruit for football or baseball teams, VCs have scouts and that go to these conferences and look for opportunities and new companies to possibly invest in.

Crowd Funding

There are traditional platforms such as Kickstarter and Indiegogo and there are also blockchain-specific companies like Weifund that are specifically geared towards using Ethereum blockchain to allow for crowd-funded campaigns (for instance). Weifund, in particular, has a unique idea where they offer a money back guarantee if certain conditions are not met on a fund-raising ground.

Another innovative company is Israel-based Wings.ai. They have a software platform that helps people easily launch projects where you can choose your governance model, number of tokens to issue, and various other factors.

CHAPTER 8:
CRYPTO JOURNALISTS, CONSULTANTS, & OTHER INDUSTRY PLAYERS

Just like any other industry, the crypto currency, blockchain and bitcoin world has its own writers, bloggers, reporters, podcasters, and YouTube video makers. I'm proud to be a member of this esteemed group with Future Tech Podcast (on iTunes) and my past work with Bitcoin.com on their podcast.

You'd be surprised at the number of articles written daily about the crypto sphere on publications such as CoinDesk, CoinTelegraph, Crypto Insider, The

Merkle, news.Bitcoin.com and more.

My estimate is that there are now 40-50 articles on the crypto space DAILY, and this number is growing extremely fast as coverage grows. In addition, you can find 50 different podcasts at minimum (a likely underestimation!), and countless Telegram and Slack channels and other forums to discuss crypto.

There are also now at least 10 or more crypto currency-related books that have been written including, The Age of Cryptocurrency: How Bitcoin and the Blockchain Are Challenging the Global Economic Order, Blockchain Revolution by Don and Alex Tapscott, Blockchain For Dummies, Mastering Bitcoin by Andreas Antonopolous, How Money Got Free by Brian Patrick Eha and more.

There are even courses in how to invest in and buy cryptocurrencies, such as the recent "Crypto Currency 101" by James Altucher.

I subscribe to several of the various newsfeeds including CoinTelegraph, CoinDesk, Bitcoin Talk, and The Merkle. It's grown already to the point where no one person could read every article that comes out about the space or watch every podcast – and the information is only going to grow and diversify from here.

The amount of news that comes out, just on individual coins like Bitcoin, Ethereum, Dash and others is becoming so voluminous it's not possible to even keep up with all the news on perhaps even a single coin. Right now, Bitcoin and Ethereum have the most feeds and of the two, Bitcoin still leads in news and in other areas, but this sector is rapidly growing.

The Growing *"Niche-ification"* of Crypto

Even altcoins like Dash are getting involved in this medium. I interviewed Amanda B. Johnson of Dash, whose sole role it is to report on Dash events, interview Dash developers, and talk about everything that's going on with Dash. Danny Somthin' of the Crypto Show, travels full time, helping businesses across the United States understand and adopt Dash.

I saw this some phenomenon happen some 30 years ago with books on computers and the internet.

There used to be a tiny computer section with just a couple of books in the bookstore. Now there are countless rows of computer books on every conceivable niche of computing you could think of.

There are books and people who just want to focus on networking or coding in Java or C++. There are those for just web programmers or app programmers. Just like computing has bifurcated into many different niches, so is the crypto space.

There now people and companies who focus on the enterprise side of the industry. For example, there is the R3 Consortium, Hyperledger, and large institution, permissioned blockchain use-case aficionados, that don't want to talk about cryptocurrencies and bitcoin.

They're starting to have their own conferences (ex: Consensys in NYC) and their own separate news channels for large corporate and financial institution and even government-related blockchain business.

Then there are the crypto anarchists, who are a live free or die, libertarian type crowd. Crypto anarchists even have their own conferences (ex: Anarchapulco) and want to be left out of government intervention in their affairs.

Crypto anarchists tend to believe that governments and large institutions are trying to corrupt the crypto space and co-opt blockchain technology for themselves, and regulate cryptocurrencies like Bitcoin out of existence... and they may just be right!

There are, of course, even more evolving segments of this industry – ones that focus on the Ethereum, smart-contract ecosystem only, and others that focus solely on Bitcoin. Other parts of the industry are segmented by the particular use of blockchain they're working to adopt, such as keeping immutable records of land and property ownership, privatizing peoples' medical data, real estate purchasing and sales through a blockchain, banking the unbanked and the remittance market, and more.

Crypto Journalists

Some of the journalists that I have interviewed include Bailey Reutzel, who traveled around the United States, meeting and talking with people about what they know about cryptocurrency and bitcoin. She has a completely unique perspective after having done so, and has recently taken an editor position with Coindesk.

I spoke with Amanda B. Johnson on two occasions, who used to have YouTube show called The Daily Decrypt, which morphed into Dash Detailed (when she decided to focus on helping spread the adoption and use of Dash coin).

Andreas Antonopoulos is part of Let's Talk Bitcoin Podcast and has written several books, namely The Internet of Money, and Mastering Bitcoin. Tone Vays is a well-spoken and prolific journalist and commentator who hosts Crypto Scam as well as libertylifetrail.com.

The crypto world is unbelievably interesting, faceted, growing, and evolving. There are now a tremendous number of people, resources and information available in this space for people to find and learn from.

Crypto & Blockchain Consultants

As I mentioned in another section, it's very important if you're going to be involved in the cryptocurrency or blockchain world to get proper business advice.

This may include tax advice if you're buying, holding, trading, or selling crypto tokens as a high volume trader, or as part of a business. You may be subject to AML and KYC requirements: anti-money laundering and know your customer requirements as an individual or as a company.

You may be moving money across borders, or across states in the United States whether it's to family and friends or perhaps as a business venture, and therefore possibly subject to money transmitting laws and being licensed as a money services business.

There are a lot of factors that everyone needs to be aware if you're going to be involved in this space to any degree. Don't just assume it's the Wild West. You can't just go out and buy, sell, trade, and ignore tax ramifications and money transmitting requirements regardless of what level you are operating at. If you're a founder or CEO and contemplating a money raise through an ICO (initial coin offering), you must be aware of potential SEC and CFTC securities and commodities laws.

As mentioned, in addition to legal, tax, and financial consultants there are also now crypto consultants who may be able to assist, some of which I had the pleasure to interview. These include James Gonzalez and Jason Cassidy of Crypto Consultant, (based in Canada), Intellect EU, Consensys, Eddy Travia of Coinsilium, and more.

Crypto Anarchists and Libertarians

One of the major niches of people in the blockchain and crypto space are the crypto anarchists, libertarians and individuals that believe too much government control is bad, that government should leave them alone to run their own lives and keep its distance.

These people tend to see Bitcoin as the ultimate in peer-to-peer, decentralized, pseudo-anonymous money. Especially loved by this group are crypto tokens that promise true anonymity, such as Monero or Zcash, and technologies that help to anonymous peoples' use and transmission of crypto, such as Tumblers, Coin Mixers, Tor-enabled wallets, and encryption in general.

These are people who believe large financial institutions such as banks, insurance companies, and government. They believe these interests as trying to corrupt the beauty of this space, to take blockchain and strip away the cryptocurrency aspect, to centralize and control blockchain-based technologies.

Large Financial Institutions, Governments, and Corporations

On the opposite side of the Bitcoin aisle are the large institutions: banks, insurance companies, governments, financial houses, brokerages and so on.

I've found through my interviews that these are not necessarily evil institutions; many are necessary, and underpin society and commerce itself.

They form the backbone of the economies of the world and they provide necessary services, such as banking and other financial services, military protection, medical care, building and maintaining infrastructure, keeping the peace (police) and more. These institutions and governments are <u>fully aware</u> of blockchain technology – make no mistake.

Large financial institutions, for instance, bear tremendous costs for AML and KYC compliance as well as the costs to process wires and remittances across borders. They need to be able to keep track of customer accounts, which may number in the tens or hundreds of millions.

They have to know at least certain things about their citizens. These large entities have tremendous concerns and there is a large amount of money at stake to be saved or lost – and blockchain may be a solution that will save financial institutions hundreds of billions of dollars.

You'll find that they are extremely interested and actively researching and investing in blockchain and distributed ledger technologies. It's important to understand that these players are out there and they're not going away. They have their own conferences and their own meetings. They know and are going to use these technologies no matter what anyone says, for their own purposes.

Hodlers (Holders)

There are also holders, who refer to themselves as 'hodlers'. The hodler term comes from a misspelling years ago that some drunk guy typed on a forum. These are people that buy and hold various tokens with the belief that, long term, their holdings will increase 10x, 100x or more.

When the price of their preferred coin/token goes down, hodlers don't sell – they continue to accumulate their holdings over time. They may be holding these tokens for years and some are now crypto millionaires. These people that think the value of tokens in their portfolio are going increase tremendously over time and so they continue hodl, for months and years.

Traders (High and Low Volume)

Just as with the stock, bond, futures, commodities, and other markets, crypto has its own markets, known as exchanges. We'll talk more about exchanges later, but as you'd expect, various people trade these markets, buying and selling tokens for profit.

Some of the traders I've met trade multiple times a day, others are swing traders. Some have even created bots that they use to make automatic executions of trades, according to an algorithm. On certain platforms, you can trade on margin, and on others, you can offer short term loans of your holdings to other traders in exchange for a small amount of daily interest.

Whales

Whales are wealthy traders or old-school crypto hodlers that are now crypto millionaires, and may have 100, 500 or even 5,000 BTC worth of crypto they use to trade the markets. When they do, because of their large trade sizes, they can make a token jump significantly in price or decline significantly. It's thought by many crypto traders that whales collude to pump and dump various coins, making their value jump 2x or more, then dumping their holdings, causing a coin's value to dip back down to its previous valuation before the pump.

Hedge Funds / Managed Funds

Although managed funds do not yet have the blessing of regulatory bodies to trade on major equities markets, various applications have been made, such as a proposed crypto or bitcoin ETF (exchange traded fund) put forth by the Winklevoss twins, and the Bitcoin Investment Trust (offered by Grayscale, a Digital Currency Group Company).

It's likely that over the next 1-2 years, one or more crypto related funds will be approved and start trading the equities markets, which will open up investment to an enormous segment of the population that currently does not have (nor want) the sophistication necessary to own and manage a crypto portfolio.

Beyond sophistication, there still is tremendous risk in owning, holding and trading crypto – partially due to managing (and losing) your private keys, theft, hacking, and poor money management.

Naysayers

Every innovative and disruptive technology has doomsday naysayers, pundits claiming we're in a bubble, or the technology is fake or useless.

Jamie Dimon, head of JP Morgan Chase, has been naysaing Bitcoin, calling it a fraud, and claiming it will fail, yet his company has been involved in scandal after scandal, fraud after financial fraud, and has receipts for billions in fines from the US government to prove it.

Another naysayer I interviewed is Radia Perlman, a highly accomplished and educated woman who has an extensive programming and cryptography background, who believes bitcoin and blockchain are just fads and are going to go away.

Celebrities

Even Mark Cuban, the billionaire investor and owner of the Dallas Mavericks, was not bullish on bitcoin until his recent statements saying that it's 'something that should be paid attention to'. Marc is now involved in the upcoming ICO called Unkrn Gold (a token people will use to bet on e-sports outcomes).

Paris Hilton recently backed a coin, and so have a growing number of celebrities. The Game, a famous rapper, has partnered with Jessica VerSteeg on Paragon Coin, and more partnerships like this are surely in the works with different celebrities.

Governments / Regulatory Bodies

As mentioned before, don't be fooled, because every single major government on earth is rapidly learning, about and debating how to regulate, Bitcoin and other crypto.

Each nation has various regulatory bodies that are determining how and if they will accept Bitcoin as legal tender (or not), require the regulation of initial coin offerings as securities, determine how crypto is taxed, who can hold it, invest in it, who can provide services to transmit it (money transmission), what legal compliance is needed to do so, and so on.

Some nations have, as of this writing, declared that Bitcoin and crypto is illegal, such as Bangladesh, Bolivia, and Ecuador. Other nations restrict mining (Venezuela, Argentina), and some are flip flopping from position to position, like China and Russia, alternately cracking down, then easing up on restrictions.

A word to the wise reader: find out the laws of your country, and keep yourself out of the gray areas, if possible.

If you're sending or receiving crypto internationally, or have customers in countries other than your own, you must be aware of both your country's laws and the other countries with which you trade, as you may be subject to the laws of each country you deal with. As usual, consult with the right professions for requirements.

Where is Bitcoin Headed?

I personally predict that by the end of 2017, bitcoin, blockchain, and distributed ledger technologies are going to be in the mainstream news on a daily basis (they nearly are, already!) With 50+ articles coming out daily and hundreds of podcasts and YouTube videos in this space, the scope and diversity of activity is truly amazing.

CHAPTER 9:

FOR BEGINNERS: HOW TO BUY YOUR FIRST BITCOIN

Even though I've sent advance copies of this book to friends of mine and business associates, the most frequent questions I've gotten in response are:

1. I can't afford a whole Bitcoin. What do I do?

2. Where do I buy Bitcoin?

3. Can I invest in the Bitcoin company and buy shares?

This book was meant to give absolute beginners, crypto enthusiasts, and perhaps even veterans a more complete background on Bitcoin and crypto. I was surprised that, after reading the entire book, I still had basic questions such as the ones above.

But I shouldn't have been surprised. After all, it took me 30+ interviews, 20+ local meetups, many hours of reading articles about crypto, and going out of my way to download various wallets, buy and sell crypto, use an exchange or two, participate in an ICO, and stake a token (Stratis) to start feeling comfortable with the whole ecosystem.

I felt stupid for about 6 months – it seemed as if everyone understood things on a deeper level than I did, and took things in stride, while I was trying to grasp these concepts.

To understand crypto, you have to participate and get your hands dirty. Now, I will not give anyone investment advice, but here is a simple way to get started in crypto and buy your first amount of Bitcoin:

1. Use your smartphone and download the Coinbase app (android or iPhone). Why Coinbase? Because they are, by far, the most seamless and easiest wallet I've found. No, Coinbase is not paying me to endorse them (unfortunately).

I use Coinbase occasionally myself, and after using many wallets, I like their interface and user experience best.

2. Register your account with Coinbase, and hook it up to your bank account. Coinbase will send a test transaction or two for a few cents to your bank account. You'll start out with a relatively low daily limit (perhaps $100 to $300 a day), but once your bank account is linked to the Coinbase app, you can purchase Bitcoin, Litecoin, or Ethereum in seconds with a few clicks (touches, actually, but clicks sounds better).

No, you won't have control of your private keys, but for beginners, I think it's better to have Coinbase control them, because the experience emulates having an online bank account

3. Don't forget to set up 2FA – 2 Factor Authentication, using Google Authenticator, and a password you can remember.

Go to Coinbase.com (not the phone app) and login. You'll be prompted to scan a QR code with your phone. Go to the Google Authenticator app, click the plus button to add an account, and the app will turn on your smartphone camera.

Scan the QR code, and Coinbase will now show up in your Google Authenticator app.

Now, when you log into Coinbase, you will enter your login and password, and then you will be prompted to enter in your Google Authenticator 6 digit code.

Open the GA app on your phone, and enter in the code and finish logging in.

YES, you can do this all from your smartphone by pressing your home button or going to a different screen, remembering or copy pasting the 6 digit code, then clicking back to the Coinbase app and either typing it in or pasting the code in.

Note: If the code doesn't work, notice that the code expires every 10 seconds or so and refreshes with a new code.

4. Now you're ready to buy your first crypto. Click the buy button on the home screen of the Coinbase app, and you'll be prompted to enter in the amount you want to buy, denominated either in fiat (USD for example) or crypto.

Ex: I want to buy $50 USD in Ethereum. Let's say Ethereum costs $500 at the time, so my $50 buys 0.1 Ethereum (1/10th of an Ethereum). Coinbase DOES charge a fee for you to buy, and tells you the market price it is offering you to buy at.

Note: You do NOT have to buy an entire Bitcoin, Ethereum, Litecoin, or any other crypto token – remember, Bitcoin and most other tokens are divisible up to 8 decimal places. Let's say Bitcoin is $4,000 and you only have $40 to spend. That will buy you 0.001 BTC (don't forget to add the fees), which is perfectly ok.

No matter your budget, and especially to ease your way into crypto, I recommend you choose a small amount to start buying, such as $20 a week. If you buy consistently for a consistent amount (ex: $20 a week each week), your $20 will buy more when Bitcoin's price is higher, and less when Bitcoin's price is lower, effectively allowing you to 'dollar-cost-average' your Bitcoin purchases.

5. Once you enter in the amount you want to buy, either in fiat or crypto (ex: $50 in USD or 0.001 ETH in our

example), you'll be shown the total transaction amount (including fees). Then click "buy" on the top right of the screen, and poof!

You will receive a confirmation in the app in 3-5 seconds. You can now see the Bitcoin, Ethereum, or Litecoin in the appropriate wallet on the Coinbase app. Congratulations! You have just bought your FIRST Bitcoin, Ethereum or Litecoin – you are now a proper 'hodler'.

Sending or Receiving Your First Bitcoin

There's one other important aspect of crypto that beginners should be aware of, and that's how to request (and receive) Bitcoin (or other crypto) from someone, or to send (pay) someone Bitcoin that you own. In wallet-speak, this is called Send / Receive, in contrast to what we just did when we initially bought Ethereum above, which is Buy / Sell.

Send / Receive

If you have a friend, associate, or acquaintance who also wants crypto or is willing to send you crypto, here's how you accomplish your first peer-to-peer transaction.

Ex: You've told your dad about this Bitcoin stuff, and although he's hesitant, he's willing to sign up for his own wallet (let's say he signs up for AirBitz, another Bitcoin wallet provider, and uses the Air Bitz app to buy $50 in Bitcoin).

You ask your dad to send you lunch money, but to send it in Bitcoin, now that you have the Coinbase app. Your dad agrees, but says: "Ok, son – what's your public key or QR receive code?". Shocked, you take a minute to think, because there are several ways to do this:

a. Your dad is far away, so you can't show him your public key in the form of a QR code representation of it, or show him your phone screen. You click "receive" from your Bitcoin wallet account in Coinbase, and highlight and copy your public key, which you then text to your dad.

Your dad then clicks the 'send' button on his Air Bitz wallet, highlights and copies your Bitcoin address from his text message, pastes the address into his app, specifies the amount to send ($50), and clicks "send".

About 10 minutes later, you refresh your Coinbase

app, and see a pending incoming transaction of $50 USD / 0.002 BTC. Jubilant, you tell your dad "thanks Dad!" and patiently wait for the transaction to be confirmed, and voila! You now have received your first Bitcoin from someone else's wallet, in a peer-to-peer manner (no banks needed).

b. Situation #2: Your dad is local, and meets you at a coffee shop on his lunch break to give his poor son some money. In this case, you click "receive" on your Coinbase app, while your dad clicks "send" on his Air Bitz app, and turns on his smartphone camera, which he uses to scan your public key (displayed as a QR code). Once your dad scans the code, his smartphone beeps, and your public key shows up on his phone. He clicks "send", confirms it, and a few minutes later, voila! You receive the Bitcoin, give him a hug, and he heads back to work.

Yes, there are other ways to send and receive crypto, but I wanted to give you a very simple example of how you can start buying, receiving, and sending crypto to anyone you choose.

As for question #3, at the beginning of this chapter...
Bitcoin is not a company, it's software and a database of past
transactions. There is no CEO, no company, no company
offices, officers, customer support, or building where
Bitcoin, Inc exists. Yes, I know this is a STRANGE concept,
but it's the norm when it comes to crypto tokens.

Instead of a traditional company with its traditional
structure, many crypto companies are what's called
decentralized organizations, where there is no single "CEO"
or president. The software protocols that run various token
platforms are themselves called Dapps – Decentralized Apps.
Welcome to the weird and wonderful world of crypto!

Chapter 10:
Cryptocurrencies and Beyond – The Many Uses of Blockchain Technology

Because Bitcoin has, by far, the most market recognition, especially to the average person, when people think of crypto, they think of Bitcoin and electronic money / digital currency. When it comes to Bitcoin, popular thinking is mostly right; Bitcoin is engineered money – a store of value, a unit of account, and a medium of exchange.

What many people don't know, is that the underlying technology of Bitcoin, called Blockchain technology, has spurred the creation of 1,000+ tokens that have all kinds of different uses that include digital currency as well as other uses.

I used to understand the word "use", meaning a use of a beach towel is to help you dry off when you're finished swimming, but nowadays, 'use' has been replaced by 'use case', so I'll USE that term from here on in.

Potential Use Cases of Blockchain Assets

This list is by no means exhaustive, but instead a list of a few of the potential use cases of blockchain:

- **Voting:** What if a nation's people registered to vote and recorded their vote on a blockchain, where votes could be counted in real time, and voter fraud was difficult or non-existent?

- **Remittances:** When sending money back to your home country (remittance), the current channels can be expensive, time consuming, and even extortionist in the eyes of the poor. Instead of going to the bank, cashing your check, walking to a Western Union or Money Gram, waiting in line, showing ID, paying a fee to send money, then having the receiver (ex: your grandmother) take a bus to her local store, wait in line, show her ID, pay another fee, and finally get the cash you sent, then having to return home under threat of robbery... what if you could buy Bitcoin, and send it to your grandmother's smartphone in Malaysia (for example), with little to no fee, in under 10 minutes?

- **<u>Banking Automation:</u>** What would happen is banks around the world and large financial institutions were able to automate their back-office processing of wires, account transfers, and other correspondence banking using blockchain technology? What if sending an international wire didn't require 4-5 hops, bank to bank, over a period of 72+ hours, but instead happened in 10 minutes? What if banks could trim the hundreds of billions of dollars they pay in compliance and regulatory fees, in correspondence banking fees, in back-office automation?

- **<u>Real Estate:</u>** What if you were selling your house or buying a house, and could see all properties for sale on a blockchain, instead of getting a realtor's permission to access their local and myopic multiple listing service? What if you could buy or sell a home, and be sure that a cryptographically secure blockchain time and date stamped your ownership of a property, so that no government or malicious entity could steal your property from you? What if you could buy or sell a house entirely on the blockchain, and have the process settle in 10 minutes instead of weeks, and eliminate the hundreds of pages of paperwork involved and thousands in closing costs?

- **Digital Identity:** What if, instead of having your personal, financial, medical, and political data harvested by large corporations and re-sold to marketers, you could control your own identity, and secure it on a cryptographically secure blockchain? What if YOU could keep your private information safe from hackers and prevent identity theft because your data is encrypted? What if you could PROVE you are you, and not have to rely on archaic methods such as national identity cards, social security numbers, or driver's licenses and no one could claim they are you?

- **Medical Records:** What if you had all your medical history in one place, encrypted, and accessible only by you or those you choose to share your data with?

What if you visited with your doctor and were able to share all of your medical history so your doctor could make better decisions about your health, instead of having your medical records scattered amongst various doctors, where it can take weeks or months to get your own data?

As you're starting to see, the possibilities of Blockchain technology are truly world-changing and extremely diverse. You can expect that many of the institutions and ways of doing things you're used to are going to be influenced, disrupted, and changed by Blockchain for the better.

Let's talk about some of the companies I've interviewed that are using Blockchain technology for their own game-changing initiatives:

Loyyal – Blockchain-Based Loyalty Programs

Loyyal is bringing loyalty rewards programs together with blockchain. Let's say you have 50,000 airline miles, a $200 credit card cash-back reward, and 2 free nights built up at hotel chain. Currently, all those perks are locked into the account in which you accumulated them –

i.e. you can't swap your airline miles for more free hotel nights, or swap your credit card cashback rewards for a free domestic airplane flight. Loyyal aims to change this!

Loyyal uses a blockchain backed technology to allow companies such as airlines, hotels, credit cards and more to allow their customers to use their reward points and (pun intended) 'shapeshift' or exchange reward points amongst their vendors (i.e. convert your 50,000 flight miles into 2 nights' free stay at a Hilton Hotel).

Why would companies allow people to do this? Currently, there's a huge amount of accounting that goes into loyalty programs, especially when company A contemplates allowing its customers to swap their rewards for Company B's rewards.

Some of these companies have tens of millions of dollars of rewards that they owe their customers, which can become a huge financial liability in the future.

For instance, if Company X has $30 million worth of reward points they promised customers, and the company is experiencing financial trouble and may fail, Company X's customers may have a legal right to demand the cash or in-kind equivalent of their rewards.

This scenario could destroy a company if there was a class-action-sized demand for compensation for those points.

Because Loyyal allows companies to barter and sell their reward points with other companies, it provides multiple benefits:

1. Customers can turn their airline miles into free hotel nights, their credit card cash back rewards into free flights, and benefit from multiple vendors, freeing up how they can use their rewards.

2. By putting their rewards program data on a blockchain, companies in a rewards network can buy or sell their reward systems, reducing their liabilities by selling their reward point obligations at a discount to other companies, or using their excess cash to buy reward point pools to benefit and reward their customers.

Because all transactions are memorialized on a blockchain, there's far less accounting and more accountability amongst companies, who don't have to trust each other as much – they have to trust an un-hackable blockchain of data and trust cryptography, instead.

Overstock.com

Most people are familiar with overstock.com as an online retailer that sells various items for your home, electronics, and more. What you may not have known, however, is that they are an extremely innovative company and an early adopter in the blockchain space. Overstock was one of the first large companies to accept Bitcoin for purchases, and has been innovating ever since. I interviewed, Jonathan Johnson, Chairman of the Board of Overstock.com and he filled me in on a few surprises.

The t0 (t-zero) initiative – In the financial world, t+3 means a stock trade, for instance, takes 3 days to settle from the time it was made.

To a blockchain enthusiast, three days to settle a trade sounds crazy. Even regular folks are surprised that our financial system still has many antiquated elements in it – three days? Why can't trades settle in one day, or even one hour? Enter the t0 initiative from Overstock.com, which we'll discuss shortly.

What happens right now when a trade is made, is that brokerages bear risk during the time a trade is settling.

Let's say you're an active, options day trader who trades on margin, and is conducting multiple trades an hour. How does a trader's brokerage ensure all your transactions settle properly when it can take 3 days for transactions to settle, yet you're trading by the day, the hour, or even the second?

How about a brokerages' entire client base, which may be responsible for moving hundreds of millions of dollars around?

If the market drops or rises significantly in a short period of time, and people on the other side of various trades don't have the money to settle their trades, or they experience margin calls en masse, a brokerage can be exposed to a tremendous amount of risk because of the t3 trade settlement delay.

Overstock's t0 initiative wants to use blockchain to record trade and ownership data of equities (stocks, bonds, etc). In this way, you could have trades settle in minutes, or even seconds (depending on the speed of the blockchain used), giving you the "t0" effect – near instant or at least, same day settlement.

This will reduce liabilities of many of the fiduciaries involved in these transactions. It will also provide transparency into the markets as never before, because the data recorded onto a cryptographically secure blockchain cannot be changed and is easily discoverable.

Overstock's preferred shares are now available for purchase or sale on a blockchain (check with Overstock for specifics). The goal is to take the t0 initiative to all equities, options, futures and commodities.

As you can imagine, being a fiduciary and custodian of other people's money, stocks, bonds, commodities, and futures is a highly regulated industry. Overstock is working closely with regulators to ensure the t0 initiative comes to pass.

I can't imagine the amount of compliance, regulation and testing that such a system has to undergo to make sure that it's workable and resilient to attack and to bugs. This is also going to be disruptive to traders, market makers, brokerages, and the entire financial industry. There are a lot of players involved and literally trillions of dollars flow around the world every year that would be affected by this.

Purse.io

Purse connects people who have unspent Amazon gift cards they're not using with people who want to buy products and items on Amazon at a discount.

You can start using Purse by registering a free account on Purse.io. As of the writing of this book, on your first transaction, you can get a discount up to 15% off on many items on Amazon.

Here's how a transaction works and why:

You, the buyer, choose an Amazon item and set the discount amount you're looking for. Purse then connects you with someone or multiple people that have unused Amazon gift cards for that amount (let's call them facilitators). Facilitators will then use their Amazon gift cards to buy the item you're looking for, and have it shipped to you.

You pay for the transaction in Bitcoin, and the Bitcoin is sent to the facilitator(s) that used their Amazon gift cards. Why would someone accept less money for an item when they have a gift card? Because, for some people, money is trapped in their Amazon gift cards, and they don't wish to use the money to buy anything from Amazon.

Sounds good, but after the first transaction with a discount of 15%, you can ask for up to 50% off an item. Why wouldn't everyone ask for the maximum discount on all purchases? Because there's a tradeoff – the deeper the discount you want, the fewer facilitators that will want to liquidate their Amazon balances, and the longer it will take to get your item. For expensive items with a steep discount, you may not get any takers at all. In the spirit of fairness, Purse recommends asking for a "reasonable" discount, but the amount is up to you

Another benefit to using purse.io is that purse acts as a trusted third party to facilitate a transaction. When making a sale, for example, you want to be sure that the person who wants to buy an item completes the purchase and pays for it, and the facilitator buys the product and ships it in a timely and accurate manner to the buyer. Purse acts as an escrow service to make sure that the bitcoin actually gets to the facilitator and the item gets to the buyer.

Purse also allows people to set up a store on their website and accept Bitcoin payments for their items. I interviewed Steven McKie, who used to be Purse's head of Business Development & Product Content. Steve told me that there are some people that are making a decent living with their stores on purse – one example he gave was of a person buying gold and re-selling it at a discount, who claimed they were able to make an excellent living by doing so.

Unocoin

Unocoin.com is a growing bitcoin exchange in India – currently, India's most popular bitcoin wallet. They make it easy to buy, use, store and accept bitcoin. They are also connecting people with various vendors in India so you can buy books and other items using bitcoin.

For a country with 100 million+ unbanked people, Bitcoin is a huge opportunity for people to use cryptocurrencies to free themselves of the burden of getting a bank account, and to allow them to participate in the mainstream financial system. Many poor people in India can't open a bank account because they live remotely or they don't have the necessary documents, money, or other requirements to do so.

In addition to banking the unbanked, services like Unocoin are desperately needed in countries like India, who are at war with cash and want to create a cashless society that they can totally control, claiming that cash is used by terrorists and criminals.

In November 2016, Prime Minister Modi partially demonetized Indian's by declaring the 500 rupee and 1000 rupee notes would be worthless in the next four hours, and that owning these notes would become illegal. People living out of the country were given a few weeks to convert their rupee notes.

In a country like India that is very rural, very poor, and has a high rate (86%+) of cash usage, it's reported that many people died because they had no access to money once this happened. They couldn't travel to banks in the major cities to exchange their rupees for lower denominations in time, or couldn't open up a bank account to convert their physical rupees into digital currency.

Not surprisingly, LocalBitcoins trading surged, and there has been a tremendous and growing interest in crypto and Bitcoin in India and countries like it that are putting in capital controls, demonetization, and trying to eradicate cash.

Thankfully, companies like Unocoin ar there to give people an opportunity to use bitcoin and to participate in the financial system that they otherwise couldn't partake in.

Factom

Factom runs a local Bitcoin meet up that I attend every week on Tuesday evenings here in Austin, Texas. Paul Snow, Brian Deery, David Johnston, and the other folks at Factom are very gracious with their time and knowledge – thank you.

Factom's business allows companies to anchor vast amount of data on the Bitcoin Blockchain (they are also going to be anchoring data onto the Ethereum blockchain at some point as well).

What's the benefit of anchoring or memorializing your data onto a blockchain? Why not just keep it in a database? Some of the myriad benefits are:

- **Date and timestamping of data** – a company or

individual can prove that they created or held a document or other data at a specific date and time.

- **Immutability** – a company's data is first hashed (i.e. a digital, encrypted signature of various documents is made), and this hash (which is a very small amount of data) is anchored into the Bitcoin blockchain. Once the data has been anchored there, it cannot be altered or removed by anyone – it can only be updated.

- **Encryption** – although you're not storing your actual data, you are storing an encrypted digital signature of your data, which, due to the math involved, is near impossible to hack and co-opt.

- **Super-efficient** – Because hashes of documents can be hashed together to make a new hash, and on and on, a huge amount of data can be anchored, using a tiny amount of space and cost. Factom is not compressing your data, it is storing a digital signature of tons of data in a super-efficient manner. You could reconstruct the ownership, and time and date stamp of 10 million documents if you wished with just one 32 bit hash.

Factom also has various projects, one of which

was with the government of Honduras. The goal is to take that nation's real estate ownership and store it on a blockchain so that landowners cannot be stripped of their land by the government or other bad actors, unless publicly done and viewable to all on a blockchain.

They are also working with the Department of Homeland Security (DHS) on various sensors at the US borders. These sensors generate data the government may want to encrypt and store, such as pictures, infrared images, or other sensor data. Factom is working to give each sensor its own unique identity, to allow for the efficient and encrypted anchoring of information produced by the sensors on a blockchain, so it can be reviewed later and corroborated to be valid and unhacked.

Abra and Coins.ph

There are several companies, including Abra, Circle and Coins.ph, that want to allow people to use Bitcoin as a payment rail or method of storing and transferring money, but without all the technical know-how required.

Their goal is to make money transmission or

remittances as fast and easy as clicking a few keys or touching a few buttons on your smartphone (i.e. Send money friends or family from your bank account through an app, in 10 minutes, with minimal fees – whether your friends or family are a few miles or a few thousand miles away)

As the user, you have no clue (nor do you care) that your transaction may hop through four or five banks, normally require all kinds of paperwork and other actions that must be taken in the background for everything to work properly. The experience, even though Bitcoin or another cryptocurrency is being used, should be seamless and simple to the users.

Abra, for example, intends for people to send remittances and have the following experience: You load your Abra wallet with US dollars with the intention of sending the money to your grandmother in the Philippines. Your grandmother doesn't want, nor can she use US dollars – she wants to receive the money in Philippine Pesos (her local currency). Your grandmother has an Abra wallet (a smartphone app), and simply sees the transaction show up in her wallet, in Philippine Pesos.

She can then spend the money locally using her smartphone, or cash it out for physical currency locally. Neither you, nor your grandmother know nor care that your US dollars were first converted into bitcoin, sent to a wallet in the Philippines, then converted from Bitcoin to Philippine Pesos. The transaction happens seamlessly, extremely fast and with very low fees.

The same thing could be said for using a credit card. When you swipe your card and buy yourself a Starbucks coffee, you have no idea how the merchant account works.

In the background, transactions are held for in the merchant account until the end of the night, then a batch of transactions is sent to the payment processor. Then there's a waiting period until the money is deposited into the merchant's account (2 to 7 days). Most people have no concept of this, and frankly they don't care – all they experience is pulling out their plastic card, swiping it, putting in their pin, and voila – they get their coffee.

The theory here (which makes sense) is that if Bitcoin use can become as simple and fast to use as the credit card system, with or without people knowing that blockchain is powering their use of money, then Bitcoin has a chance to scale and achieve widespread use.

This is what some of the payment rail companies I mentioned above are working on, and it's the most likely path that will lead to the widespread adoption of crypto.

Augur (REP) and Gnosis (GNO)

Augur, created by Joey Krug, is a prediction market, built using the Ethereum blockchain. A prediction market is a place where people can make predictions about future events, such as who will win the 2020 United States presidential election, or the amount of rainfall expected in Bogota, Colombia this coming rainy season. Other examples might be: predicting the yield of a coffee plantation in Hawaii or predicting what a particular public company's earnings will be next quarter.

Augur calls this a 'marketplace' or prediction marketplace. Marketplaces are created by a market maker; someone that creates the initial prediction and the set of possible outcomes, which can be a Yes / No prediction, or a prediction of a range of numbers or outcomes (ex: inches of rainfall). Participants can then use the REP token (Augur's token is called REP) to publicly state their particular side / prediction of that particular market outcome.

During our interview, Joey Krug assured me that prediction markets are somehow legally different from betting and/or gambling and subject to different laws, although I can't say whether that's valid or not, because I'm neither a regulator nor an attorney.

There are infinite things that can turn into prediction markets. Augur wants be the #1 platform where people can create these prediction markets and take sides. Let's go a bit deeper into how a particular prediction market will work:

Let's say John Smith and Jane Doe are the two final candidates in the 2020 US presidential election. You can see as this market develops and as election day approaches, that 55 percent of the people think that Jane Doe is going to win and 45 percent think that John Smith is going to win. With Auger, you can see the odds, based on the aggregate "wisdom" or predictions of the crowd and how it changes over time in response to various events, such as the news. You can participate in that predictive market and earn money if your prediction ends up being the correct one.

Smart contracts, based on Ethereum, are what runs prediction markets. Participants send a certain amount of Augur REP token to a smart contract address, which "tallies" their vote, and keeps track of who voted which side. The smart contract has pre-programmed instructions to send money (in the form of Ether or perhaps REP) to the winning predictors once the prediction market expires.

Over time, if you make successful predictions in multiple markets, you build up a reputation. If your reputation is good, if your prediction accuracy is better than other people, you earn more tokens from the network and can turn these tokens into fiat money or other crypto.

As of this writing, I've also interviewed Gnosis, which appears to be a competitor of Augur, and is involved in a similar market with similar technology.

Golem (GNT)

Golem's goal is to allow people to harness the spare computing power of multiple computers around the world to provide super computer-like levels of computation to solve scientific or engineering problems, or frankly, to do any heavy-duty computation without having to book time on an existing super computer.

Ethereum (ETH)

Ethereum, unlike Bitcoin, Monero, Zcash, Dash, and other cryptocurrencies, whose main purpose is to act as digital currencies, Ethereum was designed to be a worldwide computer that can be programmed to execute smart contracts (programmable agreements).

What is a smart contract? A smart contract may or may not be a contract – it's a program that is coded using Ethereum's software platform, and the code both lives and executes on Ethereum's blockchain. The code contains a series of instructions to perform one or more tasks. What's the significance of this?

1. The code that makes up an Ethereum smart contract

(or program) is associated with one or more Ethereum addresses on its blockchain. The code does not have to sit on a computer or other device to run – it runs "in the cloud", aka on the Ethereum blockchain.

2. Since Ethereum's blockchain is public and decentralized, this means the code exists on thousands of nodes, is encrypted, and cannot be modified once it starts running, unless that was specifically programmed into the code. This means, if programmed properly, programs can execute without any intervention by humans or 3rd parties.

3. Since Ethereum's blockchain is cryptographically secure, the code may not even be discoverable by outside observers, nor hackable, making it very secure.

Some examples of smart contracts:

You own an Air BnB rental home, where the front door lock is connected to the internet (an IoT lock – internet of things lock). You used to have a lockbox with keys, and would give renters the code to open the lockbox. You had to depend upon the renter's good faith, that they would not: lose the keys, keep the keys, break the keys, or copy the keys.

You decide to use an Ethereum smart contract that executes the following instructions: 1. The renter pays the landlord (you) $300 to rent the house for 2 days. 2. This transaction is noted by a smart contract, a 48 hour countdown begins, and the front door lock is unlocked, as the code executes.

Forty Eight (48) hours later, the time has elapsed, and the front door locks again, awaiting another payment by a new renter. You didn't have to deal with any of the issues described above – the code executed on its own, with no human intervention!

Another example of a smart contract:

You want a new logo for your business, and hire a graphic designer to produce a series of logos for $500. You fund a smart contract that governs the transaction with the $500, and the graphic designer is notified to begin work. The designer finishes the work, and uploads the designs, which are all watermarked are sent to the smart contract. You are then prompted to review the designs, and if you approve them, a new set of images are automatically sent to you without the watermark, and the designer is sent the $500 payment.

No escrow was needed wherein a 3rd party holds the payment. If there was a dispute, the smart contract can be pre-programmed to hold the designs, hold the money, and alert a 3rd party arbitrator to settle the dispute for a pre-determined fee.

Here's a third example:

Your company ships toys from China to the United States by shipping container. Traditionally, you have to provide the container company a manifest, listing the contents of the container. The shipping companies involve must scan in and scan out the container as it gets to the shipping yard, when it is loaded, when it reaches the port in the United States, and then you have to be notified that the container has arrived. Taxes / duties must be calculated, and the container may also be inspected.

Unbelievably, as of this writing, most of these tasks are handled by humans writing on slips of PAPER, and bringing these papers back to their office and scanning them in or entering the data in manually.

Here's how an Ethereum smart contract would handle the whole thing: at each step of the container's journey, people would scan the container, and the scan information would be sent to the smart contract, keeping an ongoing and continuous record of where the container had been and where it is in transit.

If the container needs inspection, this is done by a human, but a successful or failed inspection is simply scanned into the smart contract. The contract also notifies the recipient (you) of the container's whereabouts at each step of the process, the duties / taxes paid or payable, and when the container is ready for pickup.

ICO Crowdfunding Through Ethereum Smart Contracts

In addition to smart contracts, Ethereum has now become the token of choice for initial coin offerings / crowdfundings for all kinds of new tokens, called ERC-20 tokens. When people participate in an ICO and invest money, they send their money to an Ethereum smart contract that credits them a certain amount of new tokens at a certain time, in return for their investment.

For example, let's say ABC Coin (a fictional coin) wants to raise money, and sets up an offering, whereby investors will receive 1,000 ABC tokens for each 1 Ethereum (ETH) they invest into the company. Users send the amount of Ethereum they wish to invest to ABC company's smart contract, and the contract automatically is setup to credit each investors account accordingly 60 days after the end of the crowdsale.

Let's say I decide to invest 2 ETH in ABC coin. I send my 2 ETH to the smart contract address, I get a transaction ID (aka a receipt that I sent the Ethereum), and 60 days later, I receive 2,000 ABC tokens in my wallet, and I'm invested in this new company!

In summary, Ethereum is an amazing platform that is continually growing and finding new uses. It may even be used as a cryptocurrency, if it can scale enough to allow for thousands of transactions a second, or to be used by millions of people for smart contracts of all sorts.

Ripple (XRP)

Ripple was created to serve the banking industry and large financial institutions that move money internationally.

You might be surprised, as I was, how antiquated are the systems used to move money across borders, through bank wires, SWIFT and other transfer methods, as well as the systems used to settle stock trades, and move money domestically.

Not only are the systems used to move money antiquated and 30+ years behind today's technology, legal and regulatory compliance for banks and financial institutions costs them literally hundreds of millions of dollars a year, and a massive, punitive headache.

Ripple was designed to help automate, speed up, clean up, and make more efficient, the back office / back end systems for banks and large financial institutions.

I was surprised to learn (by interviewing Epiphyte, Bluezelle, and several other companies working in this space), of how banking works. Here's a sample transaction that would shock you:

You want to wire $3,000 to a company in Pakistan, to pay the company for a new website they built for you. You bank with Bank of America, and log onto your computer to send the wire. You pay the $40 international wire fee, and send the money. Four days later, the money arrives at Habib Bank in Pakistan, and your main outsourcer picks up the money and thanks you. Painless, right?

Here's what went on behind the scenes: Bank of America **has a bank account!** with J.P. Morgan Chase, and tells Chase that they are wiring $5,000 in customer funds. Chase debits Bank of America's account the $5,000, generates paperwork, and charges Bank of America a small fee. Chase is pretty automated, but has to vet Bank of America, and confirm a whole bunch of data in order to process the order.

Chase has a bank account with Barclay's Bank in England, and asks Barclay's Bank to debit Chase's account the $5,000 (plus a fee), and have the money 'hop' one step closer to Pakistan. Barclays, which has relationships with a major bank in the European Union, (let's call it EU Bank), now sends the money to EU Bank. EU Bank has a relationship with Habib Bank in Pakistan, and the money makes its final journey to Habib Bank in Pakistan, having made 3 hops through various banks in various countries.

I kid you not – this is called correspondence banking, and when I first heard that this is how many international transfers of money are handled, I was shocked at how primitive the international monetary system is.

I naively thought that all banks trusted each other and could simply send money from one to another. Now comes the promise of Ripple…

What if all banks and large financial institutions used a blockchain that was specifically designed to allow these players to exchange money in a trustless environment? Trustless does not mean there is no trust – trustless means that trust is not NECESSARY in order for various players to interact and exchange value (money).

Ripple is designed to allow banks and large financial institutions to exchange money faster, with no trust involved, and to exchange money worldwide, in one hop instead of two, three, four or more hops.

Ripple also promises to reduce human error associated with moving money, because of the cryptographic nature of blockchain technology, and because PAPER will no longer have to be used to move money. Yes, PAPER records are still used by many banks to document incoming and outgoing money, even though computers are used to settle transactions at end of day or end of batch.

Decentralized, Encrypted Storage of Data

Another type of blockchain token wants to improve the data storage and data security industry, such as Siacoin, Storj and Filecoin. These companies are competing with current cloud storage giants such as Amazon S3, DropBox, and Apple's iCloud.

Sia, Storj and Filecoin will take your data, break it up into pieces, encrypt each piece, and store your data on many different computers worldwide, all memorialized on a public blockchain, and all for a fraction of the cost of storing data currently.

What's wrong with Amazon S3, Dropbox, and iCloud?

- Your data is stored on these cloud services with multiple backups, so, yes, you do have some level of decentralization, but nothing compared to that of Sia, Storj and Filecoin, who can store your data on hundreds or thousands of computers.

- Your data is stored WITHOUT encryption! If hackers break into data honeypots like Amazon, your bank, or other accounts (what's the chance of _that_ happening? <lol>), your data will be compromised. Using strong encryption, and by breaking up your data files into pieces and storing them separately, you get far better protection from hackers.

- Amazon, iCloud and Dropbox terms of service – did you know that your data may be mined, derivative works made, and your own data used for profit by these companies? Nevermind the fact that you can be locked out of your own account for failing to pay, making your data irretrievable. YOUR DATA, held hostage, by these companies, and used for profit. Sia, Storj, and Filecoin are working to put control of your data back into the user's hands.

Crypto Currency

No discussion of Blockchain use cases would be complete without talking about cryptocurrency, which are tokens that use blockchain technology, and are meant to be used as money / digital currency. Money, as I've learned, serves 3 vital purposes and has important properties that make it money:

1. **It's a store of value** – the paper bills in your wallet, the Bitcoin in your online wallet, your bank balance – money is a store of value that other parties / people recognize, and agree to accept in exchange for goods or services. You can "store up" hundreds or thousands of dollars of value in a digital or physical representation because of the money you hold.

2. **It's a unit of account** – the value of 1 Bitcoin, 1 US Dollar, 1 British Pound, 1 Euro, all have a certain value, and have values relative to other currencies (ex: 1 US Dollar = 0.87 Euros, or 1 Bitcoin = $4,700 USD). Goods and services are also priced / denominated in the unit of account of money – i.e. a haircut 'costs' $20 USD, a heart surgery costs $150,000 USD, an hour of a business litigation attorney's time is worth $400.

3. **It's a medium of exchange** – When you have valid money, you can exchange it for good or services. For

example, I hand you a $20 bill, you provide a service in return and cut my hair.

Fungibility - Money must also be **fungible** to be useful. Fungibility means that my 0.073 Bitcoin has the same value as your 0.073 Bitcoin, and all Bitcoins look and spend the same. In order for money to be fungible, there cannot be some US dollars, or Euros that are worth less than other US dollars or Euros. My $100 in Bank of America must be worth the same as your $100 in JP Morgan Chase Bank. If I have a $20 bill, and your service costs $20, society implicitly agrees that you will accept my $20 as legal tender, whether it comes from my debit card, or in cash.

Bitcoin was not the first digital currency ever created, but it is the first successful cryptographically-secure digital currency (cryptocurrency). Bitcoin is called 'digital gold' by various folks, and is certainly used as a store of value, a unit of account, and a medium of exchange. Bitcoin is 'engineered money', according to Andreas Antonopolous.

Bitcoin has been recognized by many governments around the world, although has not become a full-fledged currency in the minds of many governments... yet.

Other Cryptocurrencies (Alt Coins)

Many other cryptocurrencies, inspired by Bitcoin, have been created, and we'll discuss some of their names and features here. We can't discuss all of them, because as of this writing, there are dozens of cryptocurrency coins, and the use of various tokens (of which there are nearly 1,000 others) may or may not include currency.

Litecoin

Litecoin's code was modeled after Bitcoin's code, with a few tweaks. Instead of transactions happening in 10-minute increments, on Litecoin, they happen every four minutes. Litecoin adopted Segregated Witness before Bitcoin did, which allowed Litecoin to produce more transactions per second than it did previously, even though it can handle 2.5 more transactions per second than Bitcoin due to it's shorter block time cycle (4 min vs 10 min).

Litecoin's value is far below Bitcoin's value, but it has a lot of ardent supporters and it's creator, Charlie Lee, is a highly respected individual in the crypto space. Litecoin tends to be available for purchase right alongside Bitcoin in many places, like Coinbase.

Dash

Dash was once called Dark Coin, and re-branded itself several years ago (a smart decision, in my opinion!). I personally have a lot of respect and I like Dash because their community is extremely innovative and willing to course-correct and grow. Dash has features such as Instant Send, Private Send, and has a very robust community that consistently markets the token worldwide.

I interviewed Amanda B. Johnson, a weekly promoter of Dash on her Dash Detailed YouTube Channel, and The Crypto Show, who is also an ardent supporter of Dash. One of the Crypto Show's hosts, Danny Somthin, has spent a large portion of a year driving all over the United States in an RV, promoting the adoption of Dash by the cannabis industry and by the public in general.

Dash has a smart governance model as well – each time a Dash block is mined, not only is the miner rewarded, but a portion of the block reward is set aside in a Dash treasury, which is used to fund projects to help improve the token.

Dash also uses a proof of stake model that uses masternodes. If you own and hold 1,000 Dash, you can run a masternode (a full node), and receive Dash every week or so in your wallet, simply for helping to run the network as a masternode. Masternodes also have the ability to vote yes or no on projects proposed to the Dash community. Unlike Bitcoin, which has no rewards for running a full node, Dash does, and I think this is a very smart way to run a token.

In case I didn't explain it properly, proof of stake means that individuals who hold Dash tokens are called stakeholders, and new Dash blocks are mine-able and block rewards go to Dash stakeholders, which gives people incentive to buy and hold the token. Bitcoin, Litecoin, and various other cryptocurrencies have a proof of work governance model (a repeating race to solve a math problem) instead.

Monero (XMR) and ZCash (ZEC)

Monero and Zcash were designed to be truly anonymous cryptocurrencies. Both tokens have features that obscure who sends and who receives a transaction, the amount of the transaction, and where the transaction originated and terminated.

As you'd expect from competitors, some people love Monero and think its use of ring signatures makes it the best and most anonymous cryptocurrency, while others think Zcash's technology of zero-knowledge proofs are more secure and less hackable than Monero's ring signatures.

Note: both ring signatures and zero-knowledge proofs are beyond the scope of this book, but I threw the terms in so interested readers can research them, and to make myself look more knowledgeable ☺.

Tokens, tokens, and more tokens

Each crypto and token is like a different species or creature; some fly, some walk, some slither. They all have different use cases, attributes, and pros and cons.

With approximately 1,000 different tokens out there, I can't hope to describe them all, so the list provided so far is incomplete. I encourage interested readers to review the whitepapers, websites, slack channel discussions, and other information available for the tokens they are interested in. A service that provides useful information and analysis of various blockchain assets is called Smith & Crown.

CHAPTER 11:
BANKING THE
"UN- OR UNDER-BANKED"

Several billion of the world's population are un-banked, or un-bankable or under-banked. This means that billions of people:

- can't open or are not allowed to open a bank account,

- can't afford to have a bank account,

- can't save money safely and must hoard / hide cash,

- can't qualify for a mortgage or own property,

- can't take a personal or business loan,

- can't have nor use a debit or credit card,

- can't get credit,

- can't build up a credit history

- can't accept merchant payments as a business

Being un or under-banked, or un-bankable, means that billions of people are shut out of the world financial system and are going to have a hard, if not impossibly time, of having a first-world life.

Even in the United States, there are millions of people who depend on loan sharks, friends, relatives, pawn shops, auto title loan companies, cash advances and payday loans as sources of capital to live their lives. People in these situations tend to rent, not own, and are constantly on the brink of financial ruin.

What's wrong with depending on all of the above instead of banks and large financial institutions? Because the people that depend on auto title loans, pawn shops, and other non-traditional banking are financially strapped, the default rates on these types of loans are sky high, and so are the interest rates. This makes it a vicious cycle, where a financially-strapped person must borrow money at 20%, 50%, 100%, or higher yearly interest rates, leading to their entrapment in this cycle.

These businesses would not exist if everyone had access to banking, loans, property rights, and credit. Whether everyone deserves these things if they prove themselves to be un-creditworthy is another matter.

Even for people that can have bank accounts and access to credit, or the ability to send remittances to their home country may not be able to afford the fees associated with these services.

For instance: using remittance companies like Western Union or Money Gram, can be so expensive that you can't send money home affordably in small amounts. The fees may eat up 10, 20, or even 50% of the amount you want to send back home when it's all said and done.

Lack of access to banking is a first, second, and third world problem, although the percentage of un, under or un-bankable people in many countries is much higher than in the United States or Europe.

The great thing is that Blockchain, Bitcoin, Ethereum, and other crypto tokens and working to transform the world and to bring people in poverty or un, under or un-bankable billions into the global financial system; to improve their lives and to give them access to basic things that most of us take for granted.

To drive the point home, I'll briefly describe how some of this alternative financing works:

Pawn Shops

When you pawn an item, you lend it to a Pawn Shop, who takes possession of the item (ex: a chainsaw) and gives you a short-term loan against your own property. Pawn shops have many financially-weak customers, and so they rarely lend more than 50% of an item's value.

Once you get your loan, you may have 30-45 days to pay back the loan to reclaim your property. In the meantime, you're paying a high rate of interest on the money lent to you by the Pawnshop (10% a week, sometimes more). I learned, by talking with pawn shop owners, that customers will pawn the same items over and over again, borrowing money, repaying it, and borrowing again. It sounds crazy but this behavior may be necessary when someone can't get a bank account and that's the only way they believe they can stabilize their cashflow.

Auto Title Loans

Let's say you have a car that's paid off (no liens or loans against it). Various companies will lend you money against the value of your car - an auto title loan. Just like pawn shops, auto title loans have a high default rate, and have high interest rates, from 5% a week and higher (ex: 20% a month, 100% a year, or more).

When you borrow money against your car, the auto title loan company puts a lien on your car title, and takes possession of your car title. If you fail to make payments they will repossess your car and sell it to pay off the loan you took. Needless to say, the repossession rate on cars with auto title loans is extremely high.

When regular folks can get car loans on new cars for 0 – 6%, and auto title loan folks take loans on their used cars at 20-200% interest, you begin to see how this scenario is a very unfavorable one.

Payday Loans

Payday loans are another source for people to obtain loans or money in the U.S. Let's say you who get a paycheck every two weeks for $800. Because of your expenses, you run out of money 2-3 days before your check comes, and end up with no money and no food twice a month.

You can show a payday loan company that you have a job and a stable check coming in every two weeks. In doing so, you can get a loan against your future earnings in advance of your payday.

When your payday comes you pay back the loan plus interest or a fee. The amounts you pay back on each loan may be small, but what happens to people is they get trapped in this cycle of taking a payday loan, rolling it over without paying the fees and eventually the debt can mushroom from $200 to $2,000! People get to a point where they can never even make the interest payments and can't pay their loan back. The payday loan company will then garnish the individual's wages, and now that person is in worse shape than before and may have to declare bankruptcy.

Remittances

When a foreign worker sends money back to his or her home country, it's called a remittance. Worldwide, remittances are now more than 5000 billion dollars.

Let's say a man from Pakistan comes to the United States on a work visa, but has family back home. He makes his money in US dollars (each US dollar is worth ~ 100 Pak Rupees as of this wirting) and remits or sends money back home to his family to help them out. Foreign workers sending money back home are extremely common worldwide. These are called remittances and happen in many first-world countries that send money to third-world countries.

The big players in the remittance world are Western Union and Money Gram, amongst others. Many remittances are for small dollar amounts, typically $50 to $250. Unfortunately, the fees and time involved on both the sending and receiving of remittances are incredibly high.

Here's how a remittance works: Our man from Pakistan gets his check on Friday, deposits it in his bank, then withdraws money and takes the bus to a Western Union facility. He has to travel to the location, and wait on line, will be required to show ID, and charged a fee of 7-11%. If he's sending $100, the minimum fee may be even higher, possibly twenty dollars.

The man then sends the $100 to his family back in Pakistan. In order for the family member to receive it he or she will have to walk or take a bus to get to a Western Union office. This costs yet more time and effort. When they get there to pick up the money, they too, will have to pay a fee on the $100. This is why remittances are expensive, they cost tons of time and money, and they disproportionately affect those least able to afford them.

This is why blockchain, which can transmit money cheaply, and without the need of intermediaries, is ripe to transform the remittance industry. Transactions can happen from smartphone to smartphone in minutes and for a nominal fee. Compare sending $100 to your family back home in Pakistan from your smartphone to theirs, in 10 minutes instead of 4 hours, paying $2 instead of $20. Wow – what a difference blockchain can make in this industry – and with a total remittance pool of 500 billion and more, a huge amount of benefit can be had.

Helping Merchants Adopt & Accept Bitcoin

Why is it important for merchants to be able to accept Bitcoin and not just fiat? There are many reasons, which include:

- It helps the un, under and un-bankable billions to conduct transactions for goods or services just like first world, bankable folks do. People that can't get bank accounts CAN have a Bitcoin wallet and transact!

- If Bitcoin and other cryptocurrencies are going to scale and be accepted everywhere merchants must be able to accept then easily. I'd love to be able to go to Starbucks or my local pizzeria and pay for my coffee or pizza in crypto. I also want to be able to buy anything online through any merchant, using crypto, just as easily as I can use PayPal.

- Once merchants accept Bitcoin en masse, it will increase the value of Bitcoin tremendously as a medium of exchange, and open up commerce to billions of people that are currently shut out of it

What Will It Take For A Merchant To Be Able To Accept Bitcoin?

A merchant doesn't want to have to pay high fees to accept credit cards - (currently 3.5% on average) or on bitcoin payments. Unfortunately, Bitcoin isn't there yet on the fee side, and has yet to scale to the point where its fees are competitive.

Merchants hate chargebacks - which hurt their bottom line. Chargebacks and fraud are the reason that merchant accounts (Stripe, Visa, Mastercard, Paypal, etc) see a merchant account as a line of credit to the merchant – their point of view is that they are LOANING the money earned through transactions to the merchant.

If chargebacks happen, the merchant account has the power to take the money for a transaction from the merchant, and force them to substantiate why they should get back the money for a transaction. This adds insult to injury for many business owners that can be the victim of fraud from unscrupulous customers that buy goods or services, then try to chargeback and steal the good or service for free.

On the other hand, users may find comfort in the ability to file a chargeback on purchases of goods or services they feel are deficient or problematic.

There's an education barrier and steep learning

curve to using crypto – Most people, merchants included, have no clue what Bitcoin or cryptocurrencies are or how they work. This makes people afraid to use and accept what's unfamiliar and what they've been told is money used by drug dealers and criminals.

Lack of education about the blockchain industry is a major drag on widespread adoption. There must be a consistent and strong effort to educate individuals and business owners about the benefits, uses, pros and cons of crypto.

Merchants don't get paid until days after they charge your credit or debit card – crypto can change this. Here's what happens currently: ABC Coffee Shop serves customers all day and runs their credit cards through its terminal. At night, after ABC Coffee closes, it downloads that day's batch of transactions to the merchant account provider, who then processes the transactions and credits ABC Coffee's bank account 2 to 7 days later.

With crypto, a blockchain-enabled merchant account POS (point of sale) terminal would post each transaction, as it happens in real time, to a blockchain. There would be no chargebacks, so there's no danger of money being forcibly taken from ABC Coffee, and since each transaction is cryptographically secured, no chance for fraud.

Payments would be credited to ABC Coffee within MINUTES, not days, allowing ABC Coffee to pay its bills and employees faster, and reducing its need to keep a float of several thousand dollars to pay for expenses. Sounds much more attractive, doesn't it?

Companies like Bitpay are working with businesses to help them accept both fiat and crypto. Currently, this is restricted mostly to online purchases, but is soon to be available for in-person, point of sale purchases as well.

Banking the Un, Under, and Un-Bankable Billions

We're still in the early stages of helping the world's poor and the financially disadvantaged (partially due to their inability to get credit, have a bank account, etc), but keep your eyes peeled over the next 3 to 5 years for positive changes in access to first world finance.

CHAPTER 12

DIGITIZATION OF ASSETS

What's an asset? An asset can be a house or apartment building, or piece of land that you own. It can be an ounce of gold, or a stock, bond, or futures contract. For some people, their assets are collectible baseball cards or Beanie Babies, or fine art, such as a Van Gogh painting. Other assets can be contractual money owed, intellectual property secured by a patent, or rights to a song, book, or course.

Some companies I interviewed, such as AlphaPoint, want to 'digitize' assets. What does it mean to digitize an asset? We'll cover that shortly.

Many assets are physical, and that means they need to be kept in someone's physical possession, often under lock and key. There's also a danger to owning assets that have a high value, due to hackers, thieves or other criminals who may try to steal, rob and/or kill their owner.

Works of Art - Let's take famous art such as Van Gogh's paintings, as an example. What value would digitizing the paintings bring? Let's say the painting, Starry Night, is worth $20 million. It must be kept under extreme security so that thieves can't break in and steal it.

Let's say this painting is owned by the Dutch National Archives, and the government of Holland considers it a national treasure and it wants the painting to be available to the public, so it nervously lends the painting to a museum.

Who is going to pay for the security to keep the painting safe, and for the insurance to pay for it if it's stolen? How could this asset be digitized and monetized using blockchain technology?

One way would be to register a picture of the paining with a unique watermark, record the ownership chain of the painting, and other characteristics, and put this information onto a public, but encrypted blockchain. Only the Dutch government would hold the private key that allows them to prove that they are the owner of the painting.

Now the painting could be lent to a museum, and a smart contact could be established that would require the museum to pay the Dutch Government 5,000 euros a month (for example) to borrow the painting, to demonstrate evidence of insurance, and to show that, for a time being, so long as the contract is in effect and the payments are being made on time, that the museum has the right to custody of the painting.

This would allow the asset (the painting) to be monetized securely. If the painting were to be stolen, a thief could sell it on the black market, however a buyer could look up the painting's provenance on a blockchain and instantly know that it had been stolen. When a famous asset is stolen, this isn't a problem, but when a more run-of-the-mill asset is stolen (ex: a backhoe owned by Company X), quickly determining whether it's stolen or not, and whether the person selling the item is, in fact, the rightful owner, becomes very useful.

Music - How about a song I've written? Let's say I'm a musician, and I've recorded a solo album and now want to promote my music. If I digitize my song, add in a date and timestamp, and other uniquely identifying information and record all the info on a blockchain, I can now assert that I created this song on this date and time.

I can now license my song to various distribution channels, such as YouTube and Spotify, and earn royalties when it's played. If non-licensed companies play the song, it would be easy and fast to look up the information, and send a cease and desist notice to non-licensees.

I could create different levels of royalty payments, depending on who wishes to license my song and for what purpose. If I didn't like a particular licensee's terms, either because they want to be exclusive, or they don't offer enough compensation, I can reject them in favor of who I DO want to license my song to, and I would have control over my music.

If I wanted to make my song affordable and available to nearly everyone, I could charge a micropayment of one penny per listen.

I could license derivative works of my song if I wished, and could control and monitor its distribution.

Gold - Another fascinating use of digitization of asses involves gold. It's very rare for people to physically hold gold because of the dangers involved. Gold weighs a lot, takes up space, and has been a thief magnet for thousands of years.

Digitizing gold would allow people to own it in a much more secure way and never have to take physical possession of it (ex: keep it in a 3rd party owned-vault) yet they could still benefit from increases in its price.

A gold bar could have a code stamped into it, a code that you could put onto a blockchain along with a date and timestamp, and other identifying characteristics. This information could be encrypted and memorialized on a public blockchain instead of a private ledger kept by a corporation, telling the world that you owned a particular bar of gold, and who was safekeeping it for you. If the gold was stolen, it would be far easier to file an insurance claim or to track where the gold resurfaced, or to limit the potential pool of buyers who would not want to buy a stolen item.

CHAPTER 13

CONTROLLING YOUR PERSONAL DATA

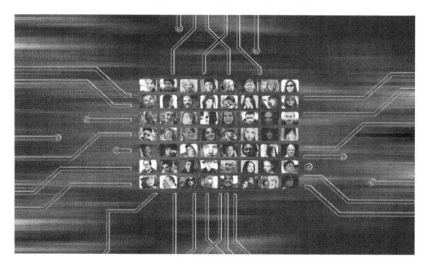

It's not just works of art, collectibles, your car or your house that are digitizable assets – your personal data is an asset, and it's currently being mined, exploited, and used to show you advertising and sell you all kinds of products, to deny or give you credit, to provide you insurance or medical care, and much more.

Several companies I interviewed, such as BigchainDB and Bitmark have a very interesting idea about monetizing your personal data.

What kind of data do you generate? Cell phone

records (who you called and who called you), websites you visit and frequent, Facebook friends, your likes, dislikes, and comments on social media. Your medical history. Your credit history. Your income tax info. Your bank and credit card transactions (what you buy and from whom), and more.

...but what if you had control of your data and could selectively share, sell, and monetize it, just like companies do? Blockchain would be a way to verify data is yours in an easy, automated way, allowing you prove you own it, and letting you sell, lease or rent it to interested parties.

This is a very unusual and interesting idea. Why not monetize data that you create? Maybe hike trails in a scenic area and you agree to mount a camera to your head and stream video or pictures for a price?

How about advertisers that are looking for people who love dogs? An advertiser could pay you to selectively share your data regarding what purchases you made for your pets.

What if a company is looking for people with Java

programming experience? You could share a customized resume for a small fee, directly with a potential employer.

As it stands now, your personal data is not kept safe, nor private – not in the least. Your credit history is collected, scored, shared, and HACKED without your knowledge or consent by the credit bureaus (ex: Equifax).

Your social security number, birthdate, current address, bank account transactions, and other information is kept in centralized databases that are routinely hacked and /or rummaged through by hackers, by advertisers, or by the government.

Wouldn't it be better to have control of your personal data in an encrypted form, and to selectively share it when and how you wish, instead of having zero privacy?

Unlike centralized databases, the unique nature of blockchain, with its encrypted data storage and un-hackability, means that, in case of trouble, you could easily verify that you are you or that your data is your data.

Let's say your identity was stolen, but you had memorialized it on a blockchain and updated elements of it over time. Using a simple legal proceeding, the thief could be challenged in court, and you could prove that data is yours by using your private key to access and verify it.

When it comes to your personal data, you want an undisputable judger of the truth – and blockchain looks like the perfect technology to help.

CHAPTER 14:
ALIASING

When you use the internet to visit websites such as www.google.com, each website visited has an IP address that looks something like this: 123.456.789.1.1 Imagine that, in order to surf the web, you had to put in a long number string to go to a website! Instead of having to remember to put in the IP address of a website you want to visit, you simply type in an alias (moniker, code name, aka) instead.

When it comes to sending and receiving crypto, the arcane system of having to copy/paste (or God-forbid transcribe by hand) a public key, leads to lots of mistakes and lost money.

Worse than an IP address, here's what a typical Bitcoin wallet address looks like: (and yes, it's case sensitive – i.e. capital letters are different than lowercase):

1TvBTSEZstWetqTFn5Au4m4GFg7xJaNVN2

Since the addresses you use are long, complicated and case sensitive, if you get one letter or number wrong or you have an uppercase letter instead of a lowercase letter, the money you send or receive will go into a black hole and never be recoverable. If you're going to be transacting crypto, especially large amounts, this is a big problem. This is where aliasing becomes an extremely important thing.

Companies such as Netki have created an aliasing system for bitcoin wallet addresses and several other crypto tokens. They take your Bitcoin public keys (which are 32 characters in hexadecimal format) and convert them to simple text format. Not only that, you can choose your alias, such as: bigdaddy555.

With aliasing, you can tell people to send money to bigdaddy555 instead of having to give them your public key. Not only are aliases easier to transcribe, people can easily memorize them, making it more likely you will receive the money you want to receive (and to successfully send the money you want to send!).

Wallet Recovery Seeds

There is one area where aliasing is in play that is very helpful to crypto users... Several wallets offer 12 or 24-word seeds that can be used to restore your wallet if the you've lost or forgotten your private key. Remembering even 12 or 24 random words is a lot more feasible and easier than remembering a 32 bit hexadecimal key.

Seeds also allow you to generate unlimited numbers of additional private and public key pairs in your wallet, which lets you give certain public keys to certain people, and also allows you to split up your crypto amongst several addresses, making it more difficult for hackers to steal your money.

CHAPTER 15:

ALGORITHMIC, ARTIFICIALLY-INTELLIGENT TRADING BOTS

Crypto Exchanges

As mentioned in a previous chapter, several dozen crypto exchanges are now available, where you can buy and sell dozens, even hundreds of different crypto tokens.

Although I don't know them all, services like Brave New Coin and Coinigy have data services that show you prices of Bitcoin and other crypto tokens across various exchanges.

Some of the larger and more popular exchanges

are: Poloniex, Bittrex, Bithumb, Bitfinex, Kraken, HitBTC, Binance, Coinbase, Gemini, Yobit, and CEX.io.

(Note: if your favorite exchange is not listed, forgive me)

Many exchanges <u>do not</u> have a Fiat gateway, due to the regulatory burdens involved, and only allow you to deposit crypto and withdraw crypto.

Once you've sent crypto to an exchange, then you can trade that crypto for other crypto all you like, but when you want to withdraw, you must also withdraw in crypto, then find a fiat gateway to turn your crypto back to fiat / cash.

Currently, Bitcoin still dominates the crypto markets in trading volume (and therefore liquidity), and also acts as a reserve currency; because Bitcoin is the most widely accepted crypto and is always available through fiat gateways where these gateways exist, people tend to go from fiat to Bitcoin, then to trade into other tokens.

When people want to go back to fiat and they're holding an alt coin (aka not Bitcoin), they will often have to trade back to Bitcoin, then send the BTC to a fiat gateway to turn it into fiat.

The Exchanges – Where Bots Play

Traders, just like in the equities trading world with stocks, option, bonds, et cetera, are now starting to use automated computer programs (sometimes with artificial intelligence) that use algorithms to trade for them. These programs are called 'bots' (robots).

Bots typically use a set of trading rules to buy and sell crypto and move in and out of positions, with the goal of earning a profit. Because Bots are computers, they can trade extremely fast and outpace normal human traders, often surpassing what's possible for humans.

However, just like with equities, these trading bots can cause problems... This year, on a Coinbase-owned exchanged called Gdax, there was a flash crash of Ethereum. Ethereum plummeted from $300 to 10 cents in a matter of seconds because a 12.5 million dollar sell order was triggered that not only caused hundreds of margin calls and automatic liquidation of many peoples' positions, but it also triggered various trading Bots to sell Ethereum, all within seconds of each other.

Just like in the equities markets, Bots exaggerate the volatility of markets by riding along with organic buying and selling, sometimes creating flash crashes and tremendous economic damage.

The use of bots is becoming more widespread on crypto exchanges, and this will have significant consequences for people that want to trade without using a bot. In the near future, it may be more than unfair to trade without a Bot – it may be impossible to get profitable results.

Lending Bots

On some exchanges, such as Poloniex you can trade on margin, or you can lend your crypto to other traders on a very short term basis. This might be for just a day or two, but it allows you to earn interest on your crypto holdings. If you're going to hold your crypto on an exchange, why not put it to work, earning more money for you?

For such short-term loans, the lending rate is quite low, fluctuating from .02% to .2% to sometimes more, but if you lend your crypto every two days at .2%, over a month's time period, this adds up to 6% a month (without compounding) and becomes significant 'interest' on your money.

Right now, 90% of the lending occurs in Bitcoin – some loans and loan buyers want to borrow Ethereum or other tokens, but it's a small minority. Again, Bitcoin is still the king! (go Bitcoin)

As you might have guessed, they are now lending bots that look at existing loan offers on an exchange, and bid your loan offer for 0.001% less, so your loan offer sits at the top of the queue and gets taken instead of other loan offers. If the going rate to borrow BTC is 0.2% and you offer 0.19%, your loan is more likely to be taken.

Lending bots attempt to front run other lenders and get YOUR crypto lent out as much as possible in a given time period, maximizing your returns.

Wisdom of the Crowd, AI Trading Bots

First Global Credit has created AI Coin, a token that will allow people to use crowd knowledge to guide this Bot's trading behavior. Investors in the fund will be able to vote on which crypto tokens are invested in and how the Bot will work, and will be supported by AI software that also guides the Bot's trading actions.

A very interesting concept – man and machine

working together, or in this case, crowd and machine.

Borrowing Against Your Own Holdings

Although this mini topic does not involve algorithmic trading or bots, it does talk about a way for you to free up additional capital to use Bots to trade with.

I interviewed SALT, a lending platform that allow users to borrow against their crypto holdings WITHOUT liquidating them. SALT will lend you up to 80% of your crypto holdings and allows you to take one, three or six month loans, with interest. SALT's platform is not ready for use as of this writing, but is anticipated to be available in the next few months or less.

I also spoke with a local company here in Austin - Unchained Capital. Unchained also allows you to borrow against your crypto holdings, although their loan parameters are different (ask them for details). From what I've been told, they are actively lending as of this writing.

As you can see, the Bots are coming, and you should be aware of what's going on and harness their power if you wish to trade the crypto markets.

CHAPTER 16

THE NATURE OF MONEY, CRYPTOCURRENCIES AND TOKENS

I don't think people in most first world countries think about their monetary system and the nature of money itself very often... unless you live in places like Cyprus – where, only a few years ago, citizens were not allowed to withdraw more than a certain amount of Euros from their bank due to a debt crisis that engulfed Greece.

Other struggles are happening in Argentina, Venezuela, China, India and other countries where capital controls and changing economies are causing people to think about the nature of money.

In November 2016, Prime Minister Modhi of India, presumably to reduce the use of the Rupee for terrorism, crime, 'black money' and money laundering, declared the 500 and 1,000 rupee notes to be <u>illegal tender</u>. He gave a four hour window for citizen of India to turn in their cash, demonetizing a majority of India's currency overnight, and destroying hundreds of thousands of peoples' lives and wealth in the process.

I think one of the big reasons people have started to think about their own monetary system and the nature of money itself is due to these recent events and also due to the rise of bitcoin and other crypto tokens. Each time a nation has either outlawed Bitcoin or tried to crack down on it or on capital flight, local Bitcoin trading volume has surged 2x, 3x or more.

Andreas Antonopoulos, in one of his speeches, called Bitcoin 'engineered money'. He said, for the first time, the human race is engineering, re-engineering and tweaking the characteristics of money to suit its needs. I agree, and that's just one part of what's so fascinating about the crypto world!

As I mentioned before, in the cryptocurrency space alone (not even the entire crypto token ecosystem), you have Bitcoin, Bitcoin Cash, Dash, Dogecoin, Litecoin, Monero, Zcash and more. Each of these cryptocurrencies has different engineered characteristics – some have faster transaction times – others are geared towards enabling anonymous transactions – engineered money indeed!

Crypto makes me reconsider how the US dollar works, how Euros work, and the characteristics of fiat money in general.

What if I don't like the inflationary nature of my home country's currency and I want to put my money in another currency that I perceive to be more stable or more valuable? What if I want to exchange my Chinese yuan for Euros, or my US dollars for Rubles?

Crypto makes me think: why can't I just use Euros or yuan instead then if I prefer those currencies to my own? Even in 2017, it's hard to do that if you live in one country and want to use the currency of another country. However, when it comes to crypto, you can 'go shopping' and choose the crypto off the shelf that suits your needs, although there are not many ways to live on most crypto tokens yet, even Bitcoin.

It's starting to become possible to live on Bitcoin (as several people have tried and demonstrated) for example. People are starting to have a choice in how they want their money to act and to behave. They can choose to invest or choose not to invest in their country's currency, and that's an empowering thing to consider.

Whether you're in investor, hodler, trader, enterprise user, crypto anarchist, crypto capitalist, or simply fascinated by this new industry, there's a lot to be learned and to experience and benefit from in the coming few years.

I hope this book has given you a taste of the amazing insights I've gotten from interviewing 200+ companies in this space. The future looks very bright, indeed.

CHAPTER 17:
RESOURCES

The Bitcoin, Ethereum and Blockchain Superconference

(coming to Dallas, Texas Feb 16-18, 2018)

To be put on the notification list

or to register for the event, go to:

www.BitcoinSuperConference.com

Future Tech Podcast

The content for this book was accumulated over 1 year's time, and hundreds of interviews of amazing entrepreneurs, hodlers, investors, traders, and crypto enthusiasts.

To listen to a particular podcast with an individual or company that you are interested in, visit www.FutureTechPodcast.com.

Future tech podcast, as of this writing, garners 200,000+ downloads a month, and is available on the web, on iTunes, iHeart Radio, Spreaker, and Stitcher.

Blockchain Edge

Because of my connections and experience in the Blockchain ecosystem, I've partnered with several seasoned marketing veterans, two founders who successfully existed / sold their companies for millions of dollars, and a team of 48 staff to create Blockchain Edge.

Blockchain Edge is a full-service business development consultancy, focused exclusively on Blockchain-based companies.

To schedule a complimentary, private, discovery session to evaluate whether you'd be a fit for us to work with, visit: www.BlockchainEdge.net or email rj@blockchainedge.net

Companies Mentioned / Interviewed to Create This Publication

Without the help of the hundreds of gracious entrepreneurs and individuals who gave their time to answer my questions and allow me to interview them, this book would not be possible.

I've made my best effort to list all the companies and individuals I've worked with to thank them for their collaboration and their time. If I've left you out, I apologize!

1. Bittunes – Changing The Way We Buy And Share Music
2. Jordan Earls, Co-Founder and Lead Developer of Qtum–Cryptocurrency Capable of Executing Smart Contracts On Mobile And IOT Devices
3. Rob Palatnick, Chief Technology Architect of DTCC–Integrating Blockchain Technology into The Global Financial Market Infrastructure
4. Neil Bergquist, CEO of Coinme And Uptoken, And JR Willet, Engineer at Coinme And Uptoken—Creating A Global Network of Cryptocurrency ATMs and Rewards Program
5. Leo Elduayen, Founder of Koibanx—Creating Blockchain-based Financial Identities for the Unbanked Sector
6. Pierre Noizat, CEO of Paymium: The First and Most Secure BTC Exchange Operating in Compliance with AML/KYC
7. Ephi Zlotnick, CEO and Co-Founder of Lucid Exchange–A Global, Decentralized Blockchain-Based Exchange For Securities, Currencies, and Commodities
8. Roger Bickley, Founder of Crypto Trading Pro—How to start trading

cryptocurrencies to make a profit

9. Joseph Weinberg, Founder of Paycase—Global remittance platform built on bitcoin exchanges

10. Jameson Lopp, Head of Infrastructure At Bitgo – Allowing Business Integration of Cryptocurrencies and Blockchain into Existing Financial Systems

11. Gridcoin, community moderator Customminer—Earning cryptocurrency through volunteer distributed computing

12. Braden Glasgow, Head of Development for Open Bazaar–upcoming development projects at open bazaar

13. Erik Aronesty, CPO of Vidaidentity—password-less encryption system using private devices to store keys

14. Timothy Suggs, Business Development Director of Expanse and Token Lab – creating decentralized applications on ethereum blockchain and ICO/token management

15. Raphael Mazet, CEO of Alice: a transparent, proof-based donation platform

16. Nick Fierro, CEO of Mimir Blockchain Solutions: The First Ever Secure Bridge Between Mobile Devices and Blockchain

17. Justas Pikelis, Founder Of Monetha–Decentralized Payment System With Merchant Trust Ratings Using Ethereum Blockchain

18. Chad Kettering and Armando Pantoja, Co-Founders of Hirematch: Decentralizing, Streamlining And Monetizing The Employee Recruitment Process

19. Kumar Gaurav, Founder and CEO of Cashaa—Blockchain Based, Peer-To-Peer Global Cash Transfers and Remittance Payments

20. Dr. Julian Hosp, Founder of TenX—Mobile wallet and debit card allowing real-life purchases in cryptocurrency

21. Dr. Ben Goertzel, Founder and CEO of Singularity Net—An Online Platform At The Intersection Of Blockchain And AI

22. Tomas Draksas, Co-Founder of Edgeless—World's first fully transparent, decentralized ethereum-based online casino

23. John Barret, host of bitcoinsandgravy.com podcast—Thoughts on the importance of Bitcoin, both coin and underlying protocol

24. Gaurang Torvekar, Co-Founder of Indorse—A Professional Network That Lets You Own Your Data and Monetize Your Activity

25. Marcello, Demetrick, and Corey, hosts of The Bitcoin Podcast-- Thoughts on creating and growing their Bitcoin

26. John Sacco, Eric Faffenbach, And Chris Bianco—Physical Bitcoin and Cryptocurrency Memorabilia Collectors

27. Jonathan Chester, Founder and President Of Bitwage–Save A Percent of Your Wages in Bitcoin Direct from Your Payroll

28. Werner Van Rooyen, Head of Marketing at Luno.Com–Global Platform for Buying, Investing, and Learning About Bitcoin

29. Kyle Samani and Tushar Jain, Co-Founders of Multicoin Capital: Managing Risk Better Than Traditional Venture Capital Firms

30. Aaron Lasher and Brent Traidman of Bread Wallet—An Easy-To-Use, Private, Secure Bitcoin Wallet & Digital Asset Platform

31. Guillermo Torrealba, CEO and Founder of SurBTC–International Bitcoin and Cryptocurrency Exchange Located in South America

32. Joshua Scigala, Co-Founder of Vaultoro – Securely Purchase and Store Gold with Bitcoin

33. Alex Miller and Karl Kreder, Co-Founders of Grid Plus–More Efficient Energy Markets Through the Ethereum Blockchain

34. Brian Deery, Chief Scientist at Factom, on Atomic Swaps, Decentralized Exchanges and More

35. Paul Snow from Factom on The Upcoming Texas Bitcoin Conference

36. Kumar Gaurav, Founder of Auxesis Group–Innovative Blockchain Solutions and Creative Enterprise Applications

37. William Hockey, Founder/President of Plaid—Enabling Innovation in Transaction Data Transmission for Financial Services

38. Shiva Sitamraju Blockonomics: A WordPress Plugin for Online Merchants to Accept Bitcoin

39. Vaughn Mckenzie—CEO of jaak.io–a real time metadata network and licensing solution for the music industry

40. Felipe Huicochea—Founder of Criptomonedas TV: Promoting Financial Autonomy Through Crypto Education

41. Tim Draper, billionaire venture capitalist and speaker at the btc/eth/blockchain superconference

42. Robert Allen—Founder of Coincube–traditional index investing tools for the crypto asset space

43. Pawel Kuskowski—CEO and Co-Founder of Coinfirm – providing AML regulation compliance using blockchain technology

44. Ken Ramirez, Co-founder of Alt36 – platform for efficient cryptocurrency payments using dash

45. Gerald Reihsen, lawyer and entrepreneur—why properly setting up blockchain companies to minimize legal liability matters

46. Douglas Pike, co-creator of Vericoin—presenting the first-ever dual blockchain system

47. Niels Thorwirth, Head of Technology at Verimatrix—blockchain security for TV networks and IOT devices

48. Oscar Lafarga, CTO and Founder of Setdev–Technology Consultants for Cryptocurrency, VR, and Machine Learning Businesses

49. Herb Stephens, President of Democracy Earth-Enabling Liquid Democracy for the World

50. David Yerger, Managing Partner at RDG Fund- The Newest In Algorithmic Crypto Trading, Data Organizing And Indexing

51. Silvio Tavares, CEO of Cardlinx–Promoting Collaboration and

Innovation Between Payment Companies, Advertisers, and Merchants

52. Catherine, CEO of Bixin–China-based, bitcoin wallet, exchange, and social media platform

53. Ben Feldman–VP of Tech Operations at Nyiax– Blockchain-Based Platform for Buying, Selling, and Trading Advertising Inventory

54. Samuel Patterson, Co-Founder of Open Bazaar—An Open-Source, Decentralized Peer-To-Peer Online Marketplace App

55. Tim Roughton, Partner at Pinsent-Masons–Thoughts On Blockchain Integration For Large Corporations And Banks

56. Michael Pole, Bitcoin And Cryptocurrency Investment Advice

57. Corey Todaro of Hashed Health- Transformational Blockchain And Distributed Ledger Technologies For The Healthcare Industry

58. Daniil Saiko and Brad Loader, Cambridge FX–Global Payments And Foreign Exchange Provider

59. Pedro Anderson, COO of Winding Tree – A Decentralized, Open-Source Blockchain Platform For The Travel Industry

60. Derek Urben, CFO of Coinigy—Aggregating The World's Exchanges On A Single, Standardized API

61. Texas Huck, CTO of Korecoin — The Revival Of Kore Coin And A Blockchain-Based Phone

62. Dror Medallion, bitjob.io: A Decentralized Peer-To-Peer Marketplace Connecting University Students With Job Opportunities

63. Steve Kanaval, Head Of Content at equities.com and cryptosumerism.com — Thoughts On The Future Of Cryptocurrencies And Regulations

64. John Lyotier–rightmesh.io: A Decentralized, Peer-To-Peer Mobile Mesh Network

65. Tatiana Moroz, Artist Crypto-Token That Allows Engagement With Fans

66. Alan Cohn, Steptoe Law Firm: Recent Changes To Crypto-Token And ICO Regulations

Token Exchange

215. Taylor Gerring - Blockchain Consulting Expert
216. ABRA – A Digital, Global, Currency-Agnostic Wallet
217. RSK.CO -- Smart Contracts Using Bitcoin's Blockchain? RSK.CO Is Making It Happen! Gabriel RSK.co
218. Factom - Securing Data Using The Bitcoin Blockchain | factom Brian Deery interview
219. Consensys - Ethereum Blockchain Development Firm, consensys.net with Arthur Hall and Pelle
220. Purse.io - Buy Amazon Products At a 5-33% Discount Using Bitcoin with Steve McKie, Head of Business Development & Product Content
221. Frank Marangell, CEO Rize3d.com, interview on 3d printing
222. Joey Krug, core developer of Augur.net - the Future of Blockchain-Based Prediction Markets
223. Piper Merriam, Ethereum Blockchain & Ethereum Alarm Clock Developer
224. Jason King of unsung.org, (Leveraging the Sharing Economy to End Hunger)
225. Airbitz.co - A Convenient, Easy And Secure Bitcoin Wallet with Paul Puey of airbitz.co
226. Jonathan Smith of civic.com, Identity Theft Protection Made Easy & Free Of Cost With Civic.com
227. Witt Erik Yorhees of shapeshit.io, Trade Bitcoin For Ethereum Or Hundreds Of Other Cryptocurrencies Shapeshift IO
228. Sean Dennis, Co-Founder of Loyyal.com
229. Eddy Travia, Blockchain
230. Todd Harris of Tech Credit Union
231. Dean Masley of Blockchainedu.org, Blockchainedu
232. BitCoin – Interview with Mate Tokay, COO of BitCoin.com